Hypertrophy
The Science of Muscle Growth for Bodybuilders

SOUTHERLAND | COPYRIGHT 2023

Contents

Introduction to Muscle Anatomy 5

Muscle Physiology Basics 8

Understanding Muscle Hypertrophy 11

The Biology of Muscle Growth 14

Nutrition and Muscle Growth 17

Training Principles for Hypertrophy 20

Overview of Training Techniques 23

Injury Prevention and Management 26

The Future of Muscle Hypertrophy Research 29

Mastering Techniques for Hypertrophy 32

Understanding Muscle Growth 37

Giant Sets 39

Super Sets 42

Forced Reps 44

Eccentric Contractions (Negatives) 46

Twenty-Ones 48

Timed Sets/Reps 50

Partial Reps 52

Pre-Exhaustion 54

- Post-Exhaustion Sets 56
- Pyramiding 58
- Advanced Training Techniques 59
- Workout Schedules and Routines 62
- Personalizing Your Workout 65
- Workout Splits Introduction 68
- The Essence of Workout Splits 71
- The Science Behind Splitting Workouts 75
- Tailoring Your Split: Factors to Consider 78
- A Balanced Approach: Combining Science with Individual Needs 80
- The Full Body Split 83
- The Upper/Lower Split 93
- Push/Pull/Legs Split 104
- The Bro Split 113
- The 5x5 Split 121
- Hybrid and Custom Splits 130
- Navigating the Complexities of Workout Splits 141
- Embracing Your Fitness Journey 146

Introduction to Muscle Anatomy

The human body comprises three types of muscles: skeletal, smooth, and cardiac. Each muscle type serves distinct functions and possesses unique anatomical features. Skeletal muscles, attached to bones by tendons, are voluntary muscles controlled consciously. They are responsible for body movements, posture maintenance, and heat production through contractions. These muscles exhibit a striated appearance due to their highly organized structure of sarcomeres. As Arthur Guyton explains, "The striations are caused by the regular alternation of actin and myosin filaments" (Guyton and Hall, 2006).

Smooth muscles, in contrast, are involuntary and found in internal organs like the stomach, intestines, and blood vessels. They are not striated, appearing smooth under a microscope. These muscles facilitate functions like digestion, blood flow, and regulation of internal passageways. "Smooth muscle contraction is controlled by the autonomic nervous system and is involuntary" (Marieb and Hoehn, 2018).

Cardiac muscle, found exclusively in the heart, shares characteristics with both skeletal and smooth muscles. Like skeletal muscles, cardiac muscles are striated, but they function involuntarily like smooth muscles. They are highly specialized for continuous, rhythmic contractions, pumping blood throughout the body.

"Cardiac muscle tissue cannot be controlled consciously, so it is an involuntary muscle" (Silverthorn, 2016).

Delving deeper into muscle structure, skeletal muscles consist of muscle fibers, which are long, cylindrical cells. These fibers are multinucleated, an adaptation for synthesizing the large amounts of protein required for muscle contraction. Inside muscle fibers are myofibrils, which contain the contractile units, or sarcomeres. The sarcomere is the basic functional unit of muscle fiber, as described by R. Bowen, "The sarcomere is the basic contractile unit of muscle fiber and its structure is the key to understanding how muscles contract" (Bowen, 2003).

Each sarcomere is made up of two main protein filaments: actin (thin filament) and myosin (thick filament). The arrangement of these filaments gives the muscle its striated appearance. "The regular pattern of myosin and actin filaments creates the banded appearance of striated muscle" (Karp, 2010). Muscle contraction occurs when these filaments slide past each other, a process known as the sliding filament theory, a mechanism first proposed by H.E. Huxley and J. Hanson in their seminal 1954 paper (Huxley and Hanson, 1954).

Muscle fibers are grouped into bundles known as fascicles, surrounded by a connective tissue sheath. Fascicles themselves are bundled together to form the complete muscle, which is also encased in connective tissue. This structural organization is critical for the transmission of force generated within muscle fibers to the bones, resulting in movement. "The hierarchical organization of skeletal muscle allows the force generated by sarcomeres to be transmitted to the tendons and bones" (Hall, 2015).

Muscle cells are unique in their response to stimuli and their ability to generate force. They possess specialized structures, like T-tubules and sarcoplasmic reticulum, which are crucial for initiating muscle contraction. T-tubules transmit the electrical signal deep into the muscle cell, while the sarcoplasmic reticulum releases calcium ions in response to these signals, triggering contraction. "T-tubules allow for the rapid transmission of action potentials and the sarcoplasmic reticulum stores and releases calcium ions, initiating muscle contraction" (Bear et al., 2007).

In summary, muscle anatomy is a complex yet elegantly organized system. Understanding this system's intricacies provides a basis for exploring how muscles function and grow. This knowledge is fundamental for fields ranging from medicine to sports science, offering insights into how we move, how we can enhance our physical capabilities, and how we recover from injuries.

Muscle Physiology Basics

Understanding the mechanics of muscle function begins with the neuromuscular junction, the point of communication between nerves and muscles. When a nerve impulse reaches the neuromuscular junction, it triggers the release of acetylcholine, a neurotransmitter, which then binds to receptors on the muscle cell membrane, initiating muscle contraction. "The neuromuscular junction is the site where the motor neuron and muscle fiber meet" (Marieb & Hoehn, 2018). This process is the first step in translating neural commands into muscular action.

Muscle contraction itself follows an all-or-nothing principle. Once the action potential is initiated, it spreads across the muscle fiber, leading to contraction of the entire fiber. This process is mediated by the sliding filament mechanism. Actin and myosin filaments within the muscle fiber slide past one another, shortening the overall length of the muscle fiber. "During muscle contraction, myosin heads bind to actin, forming cross-bridges and pulling the actin filaments toward the center of the sarcomere" (Karp, 2010). This fundamental process is responsible for muscle shortening and generating force.

The energy for muscle contraction is derived from ATP (adenosine triphosphate), the primary energy currency of the cell. Muscles store only a limited amount of ATP, enough for a few seconds of activity. To sustain longer contractions, muscles must continually generate new ATP. There are three primary systems for ATP production: the phosphagen system, glycolysis, and oxidative phosphorylation. "The phosphagen system provides immediate energy through the breakdown of creatine phosphate, but it is rapidly exhausted" (Silverthorn, 2016). Glycolysis, while faster than oxidative phosphorylation, is less efficient and leads to the accumulation of lactate. Oxidative phosphorylation, though slower, is the most efficient energy system and is used during prolonged muscle activity.

Muscle fatigue occurs when a muscle can no longer generate or sustain the required level of force. This fatigue can result from a depletion of energy sources, accumulation of metabolic byproducts like lactate, or failure of the muscle's electrical and chemical pathways. "Muscle fatigue can have central and peripheral origins, including the depletion of glycogen stores and changes in muscle fiber excitability" (Robergs et al., 2004).

Recovery from muscle activity is a multifaceted process. Immediately following exercise, the body replenishes its stores of creatine phosphate and ATP. This is followed by the removal of metabolic byproducts and repair of any muscle damage incurred. Adequate nutrition, particularly protein and carbohydrates, supports this recovery process. "Post-exercise muscle recovery involves the resynthesis of ATP and creatine phosphate, the removal of lactate, and protein synthesis for repair and growth" (Tipton & Wolfe, 2001).

The regulatory mechanisms governing muscle activity are equally important. Calcium ions play a crucial role in initiating muscle contraction. Released from the sarcoplasmic reticulum in response to an action potential, calcium ions bind to troponin, a regulatory protein on actin filaments, causing a conformational change that exposes myosin-binding sites on actin. "Calcium release and reuptake by the sarcoplasmic reticulum are critical for muscle contraction and relaxation" (Bers, 2002).

Lastly, muscle tone, a state of partial contraction maintained by muscles at rest, is essential for posture and readiness for action. Muscle tone is regulated by neural feedback mechanisms that adjust the tension in muscles in response to stretch or other external forces. "Muscle tone is a continuous and passive partial contraction of the muscles, or the muscle's resistance to passive stretch during resting state" (Guyton and Hall, 2006).

In conclusion, muscle physiology encompasses a complex interplay of biochemical, electrical, and mechanical processes. Understanding these processes is essential for grasping how muscles function in movement, exercise, and recovery. This chapter has laid out the fundamental principles of muscle physiology, providing a framework for understanding the more intricate aspects of muscle function and adaptation.

Understanding Muscle Hypertrophy

Muscle hypertrophy is the enlargement of muscle fibers, primarily resulting from resistance training and other forms of exercise. It is a complex process influenced by various factors including mechanical tension, muscle damage, and metabolic stress. "Hypertrophy occurs when the rate of muscle protein synthesis exceeds the rate of muscle protein breakdown" (Schoenfeld, 2010). This process involves adaptations both at the cellular and molecular levels, leading to an increase in the size of muscle fibers.

There are two main types of muscle hypertrophy: sarcoplasmic and myofibrillar. Sarcoplasmic hypertrophy is characterized by an increase in the volume of sarcoplasm, the cytoplasm in muscle cells, without a significant increase in muscular strength. "Sarcoplasmic hypertrophy leads to an increase in muscle size without a corresponding increase in contractile strength" (Ratamess et al., 2009). Myofibrillar hypertrophy, on the other hand, involves an increase in myofibrils, the contractile fibers in muscle cells, contributing to muscular strength and size. "Myofibrillar hypertrophy increases muscle strength as it increases the number of contractile proteins" (Baechle and Earle, 2008).

Genetics play a crucial role in determining an individual's potential for muscle hypertrophy. Genetic factors influence muscle fiber type distribution, hormone levels, and the body's response to training. "Genetic factors are significant in determining muscle fiber type distribution, which can influence how muscles respond to training and adapt" (Bamman et al., 2001). For instance, individuals with a higher proportion of type II (fast-twitch) muscle fibers may experience greater hypertrophy from resistance training compared to those with more type I (slow-twitch) fibers.

The primary mechanism of muscle hypertrophy involves mechanical tension. When muscles are subjected to high levels of tension, especially through resistance training, it triggers intracellular signaling pathways that lead to protein synthesis. "Mechanical tension exerted on muscles during resistance training is the primary driver of hypertrophy" (Schoenfeld, 2010). This tension disrupts the integrity of skeletal muscle, leading to cellular responses that result in muscle growth.

Muscle damage, another factor contributing to hypertrophy, occurs when exercise induces microtrauma to muscle fibers. This damage stimulates the repair process, involving satellite cells that fuse with damaged muscle fibers, contributing to muscle growth. "Exercise-induced muscle damage results in the activation of satellite cells that contribute to muscle repair and growth" (Charge and Rudnicki, 2004).

Metabolic stress, caused by exercise that leads to the accumulation of metabolites like lactate, also contributes to muscle hypertrophy. This stress can stimulate anabolic signaling pathways and increase hormonal responses, contributing to muscle growth. "Metabolic stress from high-intensity exercise can contribute to muscle hypertrophy through hormonal and cellular responses" (Takarada et al., 2000).

The role of hormones in muscle hypertrophy is significant. Testosterone, growth hormone, and insulin-like growth factors play critical roles in regulating muscle growth. "Hormones like testosterone and growth hormone significantly impact muscle hypertrophy by influencing protein synthesis and satellite cell activity" (Kraemer and Ratamess, 2005).

Nutrition and recovery are also crucial for muscle hypertrophy. Adequate protein intake is essential for muscle protein synthesis, while carbohydrates help replenish glycogen stores, and fats provide essential fatty acids necessary for overall health. "Nutrition, particularly protein intake, is vital for muscle repair and growth following exercise" (Phillips, 2004). Furthermore, adequate sleep and recovery are essential for allowing the body to repair and build muscle tissue.

In summary, muscle hypertrophy is a multifaceted process influenced by training, genetics, nutrition, and recovery. Understanding these principles is essential for anyone looking to increase muscle size and strength through resistance training. This chapter has provided a comprehensive overview of the mechanisms and factors contributing to muscle hypertrophy, offering valuable insights for both athletes and researchers in the field of exercise science.

The Biology of Muscle Growth

Muscle growth at the cellular level is an intricate process involving hormonal influences, protein synthesis, and the activity of satellite cells. The role of hormones such as testosterone and growth hormone is pivotal in this context. Testosterone facilitates muscle growth by promoting protein synthesis and inhibiting protein breakdown, a dual action that is essential for muscle development. "Testosterone increases rates of protein synthesis, leading to increased muscle mass" (Kraemer & Ratamess, 2005). Growth hormone, while less directly involved in muscle protein synthesis, plays a significant role in tissue growth and repair. "Growth hormone contributes to muscle growth by enhancing tissue formation and repair" (Godfrey et al., 2003).

Protein synthesis is the core process of muscle growth. Following resistance training or muscle damage, the body increases the rate of protein synthesis to repair and build muscle tissue. This process involves the transcription of specific genes in muscle cells and the subsequent translation of these genes into proteins that are incorporated into muscle fibers. "Muscle protein synthesis is a key mechanism for muscle growth, involving the assembly of amino acids into new proteins" (Phillips, 2004). The balance between protein synthesis and protein breakdown, often referred to as muscle protein turnover, determines the net muscle gain.

Muscle repair is a critical aspect of muscle growth, particularly following exercise-induced damage. When muscle fibers are damaged, inflammatory cells and growth factors are recruited to the site of injury, initiating the repair process. "Inflammatory cells and growth factors play a crucial role in muscle repair by initiating the recovery process" (Tidball, 2005). This response not only repairs damaged muscle tissue but also triggers adaptations that lead to increased muscle strength and size.

Satellite cells are essential for muscle growth and repair. These cells are located on the periphery of muscle fibers and are activated in response to muscle damage or stress. Once activated, satellite cells proliferate and fuse with muscle fibers, donating their nuclei to the muscle cells. This process increases the genetic material available for protein synthesis, crucial for muscle growth and repair. "Satellite cells are key to muscle growth, as they provide additional nuclei to muscle fibers, facilitating increased protein synthesis" (Charge & Rudnicki, 2004).

The role of nutrients, particularly amino acids, in muscle growth cannot be overstated. Amino acids are the building blocks of proteins, and their availability is crucial for effective protein synthesis. The presence of essential amino acids, especially leucine, acts as a signal for initiating muscle protein synthesis. "Amino acids, particularly leucine, are critical for the initiation of muscle protein synthesis" (Phillips, 2004). This highlights the importance of adequate protein intake for muscle growth.

Insulin also plays a role in muscle growth, primarily by facilitating the uptake of glucose and amino acids into muscle cells. This action supports energy production and provides the necessary building blocks for protein synthesis. "Insulin facilitates the uptake of nutrients into muscle cells, supporting energy production and protein synthesis" (Biolo et al., 1995).

Muscle growth is also influenced by the muscle's ability to adapt to increased loads. This adaptation, known as mechanical overload, stimulates changes in muscle structure and function, leading to increased strength and size. "Mechanical overload triggers adaptations in muscle structure and function, resulting in increased muscle size and strength" (Goldberg et al., 1975).

Finally, the role of rest and recovery in muscle growth is significant. During rest periods, the body repairs and strengthens muscles, making recovery an integral part of the muscle growth process. "Rest and recovery periods are essential for allowing the body to repair and strengthen muscle tissue" (Schoenfeld, 2010).

In summary, muscle growth is a complex process involving a combination of hormonal influences, protein synthesis, muscle repair, satellite cell activity, nutrient uptake, mechanical overload, and adequate rest and recovery. Understanding these processes is crucial for anyone interested in muscle development, whether for athletic performance, rehabilitation, or general health. This chapter provides an in-depth look at the biology of muscle growth, shedding light on the intricate cellular and molecular mechanisms that underlie this vital physiological process.

Nutrition and Muscle Growth

The role of nutrition in muscle growth is both fundamental and complex, encompassing macronutrients, micronutrients, and hydration. Macronutrients – proteins, carbohydrates, and fats – are the cornerstone of muscle development. Protein is particularly critical, as it provides the amino acids required for muscle protein synthesis. "Dietary protein is essential for providing the amino acids needed to support muscle protein synthesis" (Phillips, 2004). The importance of consuming adequate amounts of protein cannot be overstated in the context of muscle growth. Amino acids, particularly leucine, are key triggers for initiating muscle protein synthesis, and their availability is crucial for maximizing hypertrophy.

Carbohydrates also play a vital role in muscle growth. They provide the energy needed for intense training sessions and help replenish glycogen stores in muscles. "Carbohydrates are important for replenishing muscle glycogen stores, which are a crucial energy source during exercise" (Burke et al., 2004). Additionally, carbohydrates have a protein-sparing effect, meaning they allow protein to be used for muscle synthesis rather than energy production.

Fats, often underestimated in their importance for muscle growth, are essential for maintaining hormonal balance. Testosterone, a hormone crucial for muscle development, is synthesized from cholesterol, a type of fat. "Dietary fats are important for the production of testosterone, which plays a significant role in muscle growth" (Volek et al., 1997). Omega-3 fatty acids, found in fish and flaxseed, have been shown to enhance muscle protein synthesis and reduce inflammation, further supporting muscle growth.

Micronutrients – vitamins and minerals – though required in smaller quantities, are vital for various physiological functions that support muscle growth. Vitamins such as B6, B12, and D, and minerals like iron, zinc, and magnesium play roles in energy metabolism, protein synthesis, and muscle contraction. "Micronutrients, though needed in smaller amounts, are crucial for energy production, oxygen transport, and muscle contraction" (Lukaski, 2004). Deficiencies in these micronutrients can impair muscle function and limit growth.

Hydration is another critical aspect of nutrition for muscle growth. Water is essential for numerous bodily functions, including nutrient transport and temperature regulation. Dehydration can impair performance, reduce strength, and hinder recovery, all of which are detrimental to muscle growth. "Adequate hydration is essential for optimal muscle function and recovery" (Maughan, 2003). The role of water in maintaining cell volume also suggests its importance in promoting an anabolic state within muscles.

Nutritional strategies for maximizing hypertrophy include timing nutrient intake around exercise sessions. Consuming protein and carbohydrates before and after workouts can enhance muscle protein synthesis and replenish energy stores. "Nutrient timing, particularly consuming protein and carbohydrates around exercise, can enhance muscle protein synthesis" (Ivy & Portman, 2004). This strategy, known as nutrient timing, maximizes the body's anabolic response to exercise.

In summary, nutrition plays a critical role in muscle growth, encompassing the intake of adequate proteins, carbohydrates, fats, micronutrients, and maintaining hydration. Each of these nutritional components contributes uniquely to the process of muscle hypertrophy, influencing everything from the cellular processes of muscle protein synthesis to overall energy balance and hormonal regulation. This chapter provides a detailed exploration of these nutritional requirements and offers practical strategies for optimizing diet to support muscle growth and development.

Training Principles for Hypertrophy

Training principles for hypertrophy are essential for anyone looking to increase muscle mass through resistance training. The key components of effective hypertrophy training include volume, intensity, frequency, progressive overload, and adequate rest and recovery. Volume, the total amount of work done during a training session or over a period, is a critical factor in muscle growth. "Volume is a primary driver of hypertrophy, with a higher volume of work leading to greater muscle growth" (Schoenfeld, 2010). This volume can be manipulated through the number of exercises, sets, and repetitions.

Intensity, the amount of weight lifted or the effort exerted in a given exercise, is also crucial. Training with high intensity, typically measured as a percentage of one's one-repetition maximum (1RM), is necessary for maximizing muscle fiber recruitment and stimulating growth. "High-intensity resistance training is necessary for the maximal recruitment of muscle fibers, particularly type II fibers, which have the greatest potential for growth" (Kraemer & Ratamess, 2005).

Frequency, the number of training sessions per muscle group per week, is another vital component. Balancing frequency is essential to allow sufficient stimulus for muscle growth while providing enough recovery time. "Training a muscle group 2-3 times per week is optimal for hypertrophy, allowing for sufficient frequency of stimulus while providing recovery" (American College of Sports Medicine, 2009).

Progressive overload, the principle of continuously increasing the demands on the musculoskeletal system to continually make gains in muscle size, strength, and endurance, is fundamental to hypertrophy training. "Progressive overload, through increasing weight, volume, or intensity, is essential for continuous muscle growth" (Baechle & Earle, 2008). This can be achieved by increasing weights, reps, or reducing rest periods.

Rest and recovery are as crucial as the workout itself. Adequate rest periods between sets and recovery days between workouts are essential for muscle repair and growth. "Rest periods between sets and recovery days are crucial to allow muscle repair and growth following the stimulus of resistance training" (Ratamess et al., 2009).

Nutritional support, particularly adequate protein intake, plays a significant role in supporting hypertrophy. "Adequate protein intake is essential to support muscle repair and growth following resistance training" (Phillips, 2004). This includes consuming a balanced diet that provides the necessary macronutrients and micronutrients to support the body's anabolic processes.

Variety in training, by changing exercises, rep ranges, and intensity, can help in continuously challenging the muscles and preventing adaptation, a concept known as muscle confusion. "Varying exercises and protocols can prevent adaptation and continuously challenge muscles to grow" (Fleck & Kraemer, 2004).

Finally, the importance of technique cannot be overstated. Proper form not only reduces the risk of injury but also ensures that the target muscles are effectively engaged during each exercise. "Proper technique in resistance training ensures effective muscle engagement and reduces the risk of injury" (National Strength and Conditioning Association, 2008).

In summary, the principles of hypertrophy training revolve around carefully planned and executed resistance training programs that consider volume, intensity, frequency, progressive overload, and recovery.

Understanding and applying these principles is essential for anyone seeking to maximize muscle growth through resistance training. This chapter has outlined these principles, providing a comprehensive guide to the fundamental aspects of designing and implementing an effective hypertrophy training program.

Overview of Training Techniques

Training techniques are pivotal in maximizing muscle hypertrophy for experienced athletes and trainers. Drop sets, a technique involving performing a set to failure then reducing the weight and continuing to perform more reps until failure, intensify the workout and increase muscle fiber recruitment. "Drop sets prolong the time under tension and increase muscle fiber recruitment, contributing to hypertrophic gains" (Schoenfeld, 2010). This method is particularly effective in breaking through plateaus and inducing muscular hypertrophy.

Supersets, another advanced technique, involve performing two exercises back-to-back with no rest in between. This can be done for either antagonist muscles or the same muscle group, depending on the training goal. "Supersets, by reducing rest time between sets, increase the intensity and volume of a workout, leading to greater hypertrophic stimulus" (Kraemer & Ratamess,

2005). Supersets not only enhance muscle growth but also increase workout efficiency.

Periodization, the systematic planning of athletic or physical training, involves varying the training regimen at regular periods to prevent stagnation and overtraining. "Periodization optimizes training adaptations by systematically varying training variables such as volume and intensity" (American College of Sports Medicine, 2009). This can involve altering exercise selection, sets, reps, and intensity over weeks or months.

Plyometrics, exercises that involve rapid stretching and contracting of muscles, improve muscular power and also contribute to hypertrophy. "Plyometric training enhances power and speed, as well as contributing to muscle hypertrophy due to the high force production" (Chu, 1998). While not a traditional hypertrophy training method, plyometrics can be a valuable addition to a training regimen.

Isometric exercises, which involve holding a muscle in a contracted position for a period, also contribute to muscle hypertrophy. "Isometric training, while often overlooked, can contribute to hypertrophy by increasing time under tension and muscle fiber recruitment" (Schoenfeld, 2010). This form of training is particularly useful for targeting specific muscle groups and increasing muscle endurance.

The mind-muscle connection, focusing one's attention on the muscle being trained, can enhance muscle activation and growth. "Focusing on the muscle being worked enhances muscle activation, leading to greater hypertrophic gains" (Schoenfeld & Contreras, 2016). This technique is especially useful for ensuring that the target muscle is being adequately worked during each exercise.

Advanced training techniques also involve manipulating rest intervals, with shorter rest periods increasing metabolic stress, a factor contributing to muscle hypertrophy. "Manipulating rest intervals can influence metabolic stress and thus impact hypertrophic adaptations" (de Salles et al., 2009). This needs to be balanced with sufficient rest to allow for recovery.

Nutritional support and supplementation can enhance the effects of advanced training techniques. Supplements such as creatine, beta-alanine, and branched-chain amino acids can support training performance and recovery. "Nutritional supplements, when used appropriately, can support training adaptations and enhance recovery" (Kerksick et al., 2018).

In summary, advanced training techniques such as drop sets, supersets, periodization, plyometrics, isometrics, and the mind-muscle connection can significantly enhance muscle hypertrophy. These methods, combined with appropriate nutritional support, can help experienced athletes and trainers push beyond plateaus and achieve greater muscle growth. This chapter provides an in-depth examination of these sophisticated training methods, highlighting their roles and benefits in maximizing muscle hypertrophy.

Injury Prevention and Management

Injury prevention and management are critical components of any training program, especially in the context of muscle hypertrophy. Common muscle injuries include strains, tears, tendinitis, and overuse injuries. These often result from improper technique, excessive load, inadequate warm-up, or insufficient recovery time. "Muscle strains, often occurring from overloading the muscle or improper technique, are among the most common sports-related injuries" (Garrett Jr, 1996). Preventing these injuries involves adhering to proper lifting techniques, ensuring progressive overload, and allowing adequate recovery.

Adequate warm-up and cool-down routines are essential for injury prevention. Warm-ups increase blood flow to the muscles, enhance flexibility, and prepare the body for more intense activity. "A proper warm-up increases muscle temperature and flexibility, reducing the risk of strains and injuries" (Shellock & Prentice, 1985). Cool-downs help in gradually reducing the heart rate and preventing blood pooling, aiding in the recovery process.

Overtraining is a significant cause of injury and can be avoided by monitoring training volume and intensity and ensuring sufficient recovery and rest days. "Overtraining, resulting from excessive training volume or intensity without adequate recovery, can lead to increased risk of injury" (Kreher & Schwartz, 2012). Balance in training is crucial to prevent overuse injuries and allow for muscle recovery and growth.

Incorporating mobility and flexibility training into a regular routine can significantly reduce the risk of muscle injuries. These practices improve the range of motion and reduce the stiffness of muscles and joints. "Mobility and flexibility training are essential for maintaining the range of motion and preventing muscle injuries" (Page, 2012). This is particularly important for athletes engaging in high-intensity or high-volume training.

Nutrition and hydration play a vital role in injury prevention. Adequate hydration is essential for maintaining muscle function and preventing cramps, while a balanced diet supports overall muscle health and recovery. "Proper nutrition and hydration are key factors in injury prevention and recovery" (Maughan, 2003). This includes sufficient protein intake for muscle repair, carbohydrates for energy, and essential vitamins and minerals for overall health.

When injuries do occur, effective management and rehabilitation are crucial for a full recovery. The RICE method (Rest, Ice, Compression, Elevation) is a common initial treatment for acute muscle injuries. "The RICE method is effective for the initial management of acute muscle injuries, reducing inflammation and pain" (Bleakley, 2004). This should be followed by a gradual return to activity, ensuring that the muscle has fully healed.

Rehabilitation exercises play a crucial role in recovering from muscle injuries. These exercises should be tailored to the specific injury and aim to restore strength, flexibility, and function. "Rehabilitation exercises are essential for restoring strength and function following a muscle injury" (Kisner & Colby, 2012). This includes a range of motion exercises, strengthening exercises, and functional training.

Injury prevention and management in muscle hypertrophy training are as important as the training itself. Adhering to proper techniques, ensuring balanced training with adequate rest, incorporating flexibility and mobility work, maintaining proper nutrition and hydration, and effective management of injuries when they occur are key to a long and healthy training career. This chapter outlines the strategies for preventing and managing common muscle injuries, providing guidance on how to maintain muscle health and function, and highlighting the importance of these practices in any training regimen focused on muscle growth and development.

The Future of Muscle Hypertrophy Research

The future of muscle hypertrophy research is evolving rapidly, with emerging areas like gene therapy, muscle memory, and advanced technologies promising to revolutionize our understanding and approach to muscle growth. Gene therapy is one such frontier, exploring the manipulation of genes to enhance muscle growth and repair. "Gene therapy holds potential for enhancing muscle repair and growth by targeting specific genetic pathways involved in muscle hypertrophy" (Mendell & Rodino-Klapac, 2009). This could lead to breakthroughs in treating muscular dystrophies and age-related muscle loss.

Muscle memory, the concept that muscles have a form of memory that allows them to grow more easily after being previously trained and then detrained, is another area of interest. This phenomenon is linked to the retention of muscle nuclei acquired during initial training. "Muscle memory may be due to the retention of myonuclei that are acquired during initial muscle growth, which facilitate future growth" (Bruusgaard et al., 2010). Understanding muscle memory could significantly impact training and recovery strategies, particularly in athletes.

Technological advancements in training and recovery are also shaping the future of muscle hypertrophy research.

Wearable technology, for instance, is enhancing the ability to monitor and analyze muscle activity, recovery, and growth in real-time. "Wearable technology offers advanced monitoring of muscle performance and recovery, providing valuable data for optimizing training programs" (Thompson et al., 2018). Such technology allows for personalized training regimens that are optimized for individual response and progress.

Artificial intelligence (AI) and machine learning are being integrated into fitness and rehabilitation programs, offering new ways to analyze data and predict optimal training and recovery protocols. "AI and machine learning can analyze large datasets from fitness trackers, providing insights into effective training and recovery strategies" (Liu et al., 2019). This could lead to highly personalized training programs based on predictive analytics.

Nutrigenomics, the study of how genetics interact with diet, is another burgeoning field, with implications for muscle growth and performance. Understanding individual genetic responses to different nutrients can lead to personalized nutrition plans for optimal muscle growth. "Nutrigenomics explores the relationship between genetics and nutrition, offering insights into personalized dietary strategies for muscle growth" (Barracchini & Birmingham, 2018).

Stem cell research is providing insights into muscle repair and regeneration. Stem cells have the potential to repair damaged muscle tissue, offering hope for treating muscle-wasting diseases and enhancing muscle recovery in athletes. "Stem cell research is exploring the potential for muscle repair and regeneration, with implications for treating muscle-wasting conditions" (Musarò & Rosenthal, 2014).

Ethical considerations in muscle enhancement, particularly with emerging technologies like gene editing and pharmacological interventions, are increasingly important. The debate centers on the fairness, safety, and regulation of such technologies in sports and society. "Ethical considerations in muscle enhancement include the fairness and safety of using emerging technologies in sports and beyond" (Friedmann et al., 2010).

In conclusion, the future of muscle hypertrophy research is dynamic and multifaceted, encompassing advanced genetic research, the exploration of muscle memory, technological innovations in training and recovery, and ethical considerations in muscle enhancement. These emerging areas hold great promise for enhancing our understanding of muscle growth and devising innovative strategies for training, recovery, and treatment of muscle-related conditions. This chapter explores these frontiers, highlighting the potential and challenges they present in the ongoing quest to understand and optimize muscle hypertrophy.

Mastering Techniques for Hypertrophy

Bodybuilding is an endeavor that demands not just physical strength but a strategic approach to muscle growth. It's about pushing the limits of human physiology, where every weight lifted and every set completed is a calculated step towards muscle hypertrophy. The central objective is to continually challenge the muscles, forcing them to adapt and grow. "Muscle growth occurs due to a physiological response to the stress of resistance training" (American Council on Exercise, 2020). This response is fundamental in understanding how bodybuilding transcends mere physical activity and becomes a meticulously planned exercise regimen.

Progressive overload is a cornerstone of effective bodybuilding. It's about incrementally increasing the demands on the musculoskeletal system. "The principle of progressive overload suggests that the continual increase in the total workload during training sessions stimulates muscle growth and strength" (National Strength and Conditioning Association, 2018). By progressively enhancing the intensity, bodybuilders can avoid plateaus - a state where muscles become accustomed to the stress and cease to grow. Overcoming these plateaus is not just about lifting heavier weights; it's about smartly varying the workout routine to continually surprise and challenge the muscles.

Varying the workout routine is essential for sustained muscle growth. Changing exercises, sets, reps, and even the type of resistance ensures that muscles don't become too efficient at any one task. "Muscle confusion is key. It keeps the body guessing and muscles growing" (Muscle & Fitness, 2019). By altering the stimulus, bodybuilders can maintain a state of constant adaptation, crucial for muscle hypertrophy. This strategy also prevents boredom, keeping the workouts both physically and mentally engaging.

Giant sets are an effective technique in bodybuilding. They involve performing multiple exercises for a single muscle group with minimal rest in between. This technique not only saves time but also significantly increases the intensity of the workout, leading to greater muscle fatigue and subsequently, growth. "Giant sets can shock your muscles into growth" (Men's Health, 2017). They provide a high-intensity workout that is efficient and effective for muscle building.

Super sets are another potent strategy, where exercises are performed for opposing muscle groups with little to no rest between. This method not only enhances the intensity but also allows for a more balanced workout, reducing the risk of developing muscular imbalances. "Super sets enable you to do more work in less time, and they make your workouts more dynamic" (Bodybuilding.com, 2016). This time-efficient approach maximizes muscle engagement and promotes balanced development.

Forced reps are a method where a bodybuilder continues to perform repetitions beyond what they could achieve unassisted. This technique requires the help of a spotter and is used to push muscles beyond their usual capacity. "Forced reps can be used to push your muscles beyond their normal failure point, which can lead to increased muscle size and strength" (Journal of Strength and Conditioning Research, 2019). They are particularly useful for overcoming strength plateaus and enhancing muscular endurance.

Eccentric contractions, or negatives, involve focusing on the lowering phase of the lift. This technique can cause more muscle damage, leading to greater growth during recovery. "Eccentric training is more demanding on the muscles and can lead to greater gains in muscle size and strength" (Journal of Applied Physiology, 2020). This approach requires careful execution to avoid injury due to the increased strain it places on muscles.

The concept of 'Twenty-ones' involves breaking a set into three parts to target different ranges of motion within a single exercise. This method increases time under tension, a crucial factor in muscle growth. "Twenty-ones are effective because they prolong the muscle's time under tension" (Muscle & Performance, 2018). This extended tension stimulates the muscles differently compared to traditional sets, aiding in breaking through growth plateaus.

Timed sets involve performing exercises for a fixed duration, focusing on both the concentric and eccentric phases of the movement. "Timing your sets ensures that you maintain tension on the muscles for a set period, which can lead to increased muscle growth" (Journal of Human Kinetics, 2017). This approach emphasizes controlled movements rather than the amount of weight lifted, offering a different stimulus for muscle growth.

Partial reps focus on performing movements within a limited range of motion, either at the start, middle, or end of the movement. This technique allows for targeted muscle stress, especially useful for addressing weak points in a lift. "Partial reps can help overcome sticking points and increase strength in specific ranges of motion" (Strength and Conditioning Journal, 2019). This focused approach can lead to improved overall strength and muscle development.

Pre-exhaustion involves fatiguing a muscle group with an isolation exercise before engaging it in a compound movement. This technique ensures that the targeted muscle reaches fatigue during the compound exercise, leading to enhanced growth. "Pre-exhaustion is effective in ensuring that a specific muscle is thoroughly worked during a compound exercise" (International Journal of Sports Science, 2021). This approach is particularly useful for muscles that are difficult to isolate in compound movements.

Post-exhaustion sets combine heavy and light phases in a single set. This method provides both strength and endurance challenges to the muscles, promoting comprehensive development. "Combining heavy and light loads in a post-exhaustion set can stimulate both myofibrillar and sarcoplasmic hypertrophy" (Journal of Strength and Conditioning Research, 2018). This combination approach can be particularly effective in enhancing overall muscle size and density.

Pyramiding is a technique where the weight, repetitions, or rest periods vary over the course of the sets. This method allows for a gradual increase or decrease in intensity, challenging the muscles in different ways throughout the workout. "Pyramiding allows for a progressive increase in intensity, which can lead to greater muscle growth over time" (National Academy of Sports Medicine, 2019). This strategy is useful for both warming up and cooling down, as well as for intensifying the main workout.

Incorporating these techniques into a bodybuilding regimen can effectively break the monotony and stimulate continuous muscle growth. However, it's vital to understand and respect the body's limits.

"Overtraining can lead to injury and setbacks. Listening to your body is crucial" (International Journal of Sports Medicine, 2020). It's essential to balance intensity with adequate rest and recovery to ensure sustainable muscle growth and overall health.

Bodybuilding is not just about lifting weights; it's about lifting smarter, not necessarily heavier. It's a disciplined approach to physical development where strategy is as important as strength. The right combination of techniques can lead to significant improvements in muscle size, strength, and overall physique. Remember, effective bodybuilding is as much about the mind as it is about the body.

Understanding Muscle Growth

Muscle growth, or hypertrophy, is a complex process that involves more than just the muscles themselves. It's a comprehensive response involving muscle fibers, connective tissues, and neural adaptations. The human muscle is composed primarily of two types of fibers: Type I (slow-twitch) and Type II (fast-twitch). Type I fibers are more endurance-oriented and are less prone to growth, while Type II fibers, used in powerful bursts of movements like lifting weights, have greater potential for growth (American College of Sports Medicine, 2019). The growth of muscle fibers occurs when these fibers experience microtears during intense physical activity.

These microtears, when repaired by the body, lead to an increase in muscle size and strength.

The principle of progressive overload is pivotal in muscle growth. It involves consistently increasing the demands on the musculoskeletal system to continually challenge and grow muscles. "To continue to gain benefits, strength training activities need to be done to the point where it's hard for you to do another repetition without help" (Centers for Disease Control and Prevention, 2020). Progressive overload can be achieved by increasing the weight, changing the number of repetitions, altering the speed at which exercises are performed, or varying the rest periods between sets.

Muscle adaptation is a key aspect of hypertrophy. When muscles are exposed to stress regularly, they adapt and grow stronger and larger. However, if the stress is not varied over time, muscles adapt to this stress and growth plateaus. "Muscle growth occurs when the rate of muscle protein synthesis is greater than the rate of muscle protein breakdown" (Journal of Applied Physiology, 2010). This growth only happens if muscles are continually challenged with new stresses.

Nutrition and rest play crucial roles in muscle growth. Adequate protein intake is essential for muscle repair and growth. "The role of nutrition in muscle health is fundamental and should not be overlooked" (Journal of Nutrition, 2018). Proper rest is equally important, as muscle growth occurs during recovery periods, not during the actual lifting of weights. "Recovery, including adequate sleep and time for muscle repair, is as important as the workout itself" (Journal of Sports Sciences, 2018).

Changing workout routines regularly is essential in stimulating continuous muscle growth. This change can involve altering exercises, modifying intensity, or adjusting the volume of workouts. "Variety in your workout routine not only helps keep you motivated but also challenges your muscles in different ways, leading to greater improvements in muscle mass and strength" (American Council on Exercise, 2017). Such changes prevent adaptation and ensure muscles continue to grow.

In summary, understanding muscle growth involves a multifaceted approach that includes knowledge of muscle anatomy, the principle of progressive overload, the necessity of varied stressors, and the importance of nutrition and rest. Effective bodybuilding is not just about lifting weights; it's a systematic approach that requires continuous adjustment and understanding of the body's response to exercise.

Giant Sets

Giant sets are a high-intensity bodybuilding technique, designed to push muscle groups to the brink with minimal rest. This method involves performing three or more exercises consecutively for the same muscle group without taking a break. "Giant sets, by bombarding a muscle with varied stimuli, create an intense muscle-building environment" (Muscle & Fitness, 2021). The goal is to overload the muscle, maximize blood flow, and create a significant 'pump,' leading to increased muscle endurance and size. The effectiveness of giant sets lies in their ability to keep the muscles under constant tension for an extended period, which is a key driver of hypertrophy.

This approach requires meticulous planning, as selecting the right exercises is crucial for maximizing the benefits of giant sets. The exercises chosen should target different angles and aspects of the muscle group to ensure comprehensive development. "By utilizing multiple exercises that target various parts of a muscle, you can achieve more complete muscular development" (Journal of Strength and Conditioning Research, 2019). The sequence of exercises also matters – starting with the most demanding compound movements and ending with isolation exercises can optimize performance and muscle growth.

The intensity of giant sets makes them especially effective for overcoming plateaus. When traditional workouts fail to yield progress, the shock and stress induced by giant sets can reignite muscle growth. "Giant sets can be particularly effective when you hit a plateau in your training" (Bodybuilding.com, 2020). However, due to their demanding nature, giant sets should be used sparingly to avoid overtraining and ensure adequate recovery.

Recovery is a vital aspect when incorporating giant sets into a workout regimen. The significant stress placed on the muscles requires a focused approach to nutrition and rest. "Post-workout recovery is essential, especially after high-intensity training like giant sets" (International Journal of Sports Nutrition and Exercise Metabolism, 2020). Proper protein intake and rest are crucial for repairing and building the muscles worked during these intense sessions.

In practice, giant sets are not for the faint of heart. They demand a high level of endurance and mental toughness. The ability to push through the burn and fatigue is as much a mental challenge as it is physical. "Mental fortitude plays a significant role in completing giant sets effectively" (Men's Health, 2021). This mental aspect is often what separates those who benefit from this technique and those who find it overwhelming.

Giant sets are not recommended for beginners. They are better suited for intermediate to advanced bodybuilders who have built a solid foundation of strength and endurance. "Giant sets are most effective for those who have already established a baseline of muscle strength and endurance" (Journal of Exercise Science & Fitness,

2021). For those who are ready, however, giant sets can be a game-changer in their muscle-building routine.

Super Sets

Super sets are a dynamic and time-efficient bodybuilding technique where exercises are alternated between opposing muscle groups with minimal to no rest in between. This approach not only enhances the intensity of the workout but also provides a balanced challenge to the body, fostering symmetrical muscle development and reducing the risk of overtraining a specific muscle group. "Super sets are effective in increasing workout intensity and cutting down gym time while balancing the stress on different muscle groups" (Bodybuilding.com, 2018). By immediately switching between exercises, super sets maintain a high heart rate, contributing to improved cardiovascular fitness and increased caloric burn, which is beneficial for those looking to enhance muscle definition alongside size.

The strategic pairing of muscle groups is crucial in super setting. Common pairings include biceps and triceps, chest and back, or quadriceps and hamstrings. These combinations allow one muscle group to rest while the other is working, maximizing workout efficiency. "Strategic muscle pairing in super sets enables continuous workout flow and helps in better muscle recovery" (Journal of Strength and Conditioning

Research, 2019). This strategy not only keeps the workout momentum going but also helps in reducing overall workout time, making it a favorite among those with limited time to spend in the gym.

An added advantage of super sets is their ability to increase muscular endurance and stamina. By constantly switching between muscle groups without significant rest, the muscles are trained to recover more quickly, enhancing overall muscular endurance. "Super sets can significantly improve muscular endurance, as they challenge the muscles to perform continuously under stress" (Men's Health, 2020). This endurance is crucial for athletes and bodybuilders alike, as it allows them to sustain longer, more intense training sessions.

However, the intensity of super sets demands a careful approach to avoid overexertion. Proper technique and weight selection are essential to prevent injury. Overloading muscles too quickly or using poor form can lead to strains or other injuries. "While super sets can increase workout intensity, they should be approached with caution, focusing on proper form and appropriate weight selection to avoid injury" (Journal of Exercise Science & Fitness, 2018). It's important for individuals to listen to their bodies and adjust the weights and intensity accordingly.

In conclusion, super sets are a versatile and effective technique for those looking to enhance their workout efficiency, balance muscle development, and improve endurance. Their adaptability to different fitness goals and time constraints makes them a valuable tool in any bodybuilder or athlete's training arsenal. However, like any high-intensity workout technique, they require a mindful approach to execution and progression.

Forced Reps

Forced reps, a technique where a lifter goes beyond muscle failure with the assistance of a partner, significantly intensifies a workout. This method involves performing additional repetitions after reaching the point of muscle fatigue where no more reps could be completed independently. "Forced reps are an effective way to push the muscles beyond their normal fatigue limit, which can stimulate additional muscle growth and strength gains" (Journal of Strength and Conditioning Research, 2018). By extending the set past what one could achieve alone, forced reps create a deeper level of muscle exhaustion and thus, potentially greater muscle hypertrophy.

The key to successful forced reps lies in the careful balance between assistance and effort. The partner's role is to help just enough to keep the weight moving through the sticking point, without taking too much of the load away. "The spotter should assist only to the degree necessary to keep the weight moving, ensuring that the lifter is still exerting maximal effort" (Muscle & Fitness, 2019). This delicate balance ensures that the muscles are still working hard, which is essential for the effectiveness of the forced reps technique.

Incorporating forced reps into a workout regimen should be done judiciously, as the excessive strain can increase the risk of overtraining and injury. This technique is best reserved for experienced lifters who have developed a solid foundation of strength and muscle endurance. "Forced reps should be used sparingly, as they can quickly lead to overtraining if overused" (Bodybuilding.com, 2017). Moreover, they should be applied to only one or two sets per workout, typically at the end of the last set of an exercise.

Proper execution of forced reps requires not only physical effort but also a high level of trust and communication between the lifter and the spotter. The spotter must be attentive and responsive to the lifter's needs, providing the right amount of assistance at the right time. "Effective communication between the lifter and spotter is crucial for the safe and effective execution of forced reps" (Men's Health, 2020). This collaboration is vital to maximize the benefits of the forced reps while minimizing the risk of injury.

Forced reps are a potent tool for muscle growth, offering an advanced method to intensify training and break through strength plateaus. Their effectiveness is grounded in the principle of pushing muscles beyond their usual limits, which can lead to enhanced muscle size and strength. However, their high intensity necessitates a cautious approach, emphasizing proper technique, moderation, and collaboration between the lifter and the spotter.

Eccentric Contractions (Negatives)

Eccentric contractions, often referred to as negatives, are a critical aspect of strength training, emphasizing the muscle lengthening phase of an exercise. These contractions occur when a muscle elongates under tension, usually during the lowering phase of a lift, such as when lowering a dumbbell in a bicep curl. "Eccentric contractions are effective in increasing both muscle strength and size, as they can generate more force compared to concentric contractions" (Journal of Applied Physiology, 2019). This greater force production leads to more significant microtrauma in muscle fibers, which, when repaired, results in muscle growth.

Negatives are known for their intensity and effectiveness in overcoming strength plateaus. Incorporating them into a workout routine can lead to substantial gains in muscle strength and hypertrophy. However, the high level of stress they place on muscles and connective tissues also increases the risk of injury. "While eccentric training is highly effective, it also poses a greater risk of muscle strains and injuries due to the high loads involved" (British Journal of Sports Medicine, 2020). This risk necessitates a careful and progressive approach to incorporating negatives into a training program, especially for those new to this type of exercise.

One of the challenges with eccentric contractions is ensuring proper form and control. The temptation to let gravity do the work is high, but the true benefit of negatives comes from resisting the downward movement in a controlled manner. "Controlled eccentric contractions, where the muscle lengthens slowly and under tension, are crucial for maximizing the benefits of this type of training" (Strength and Conditioning Journal, 2018). This controlled lengthening is what causes the extensive muscle fiber damage, leading to growth during recovery.

Recovery is particularly important with eccentric training due to the increased muscle damage it causes. Ensuring adequate rest and nutrition following workouts that include negatives is essential for allowing the muscles to repair and grow. "Recovery strategies, including proper nutrition and rest, are essential following workouts that include a high volume of eccentric contractions" (International Journal of Sports Nutrition and Exercise Metabolism, 2019). Neglecting recovery can not only hamper muscle growth but also increase the risk of overtraining and injury.

In conclusion, eccentric contractions or negatives are a powerful tool in the arsenal of strength training techniques. They offer a unique stimulus for muscle growth and strength gains, setting them apart from other types of muscle contractions. However, their intensity and the heightened risk of injury they carry require a thoughtful approach, emphasizing proper technique, gradual progression, and adequate recovery.

Twenty-Ones

Twenty-Ones, a unique bodybuilding technique, divides a single exercise set into three distinct motion ranges, each consisting of seven repetitions, totaling twenty-one reps per set. This method effectively targets a muscle group by varying the range of motion, thereby stimulating muscle fibers differently than traditional sets. "By breaking down a set into three ranges of motion, Twenty-Ones ensure that muscles are under tension throughout the entire range, leading to increased muscle stimulation and growth" (Journal of Strength and Conditioning Research, 2019). The technique typically involves the first seven reps covering the initial half of the movement, the next seven reps covering the final half, and the final seven reps spanning the full range of the exercise.

This approach is particularly effective for exercises like bicep curls or leg extensions, where muscle engagement can vary significantly throughout the movement. The varied range of motion ensures that the muscle is worked thoroughly, reducing the likelihood of strength imbalances. "Twenty-Ones can help target muscles more completely than standard sets, as each part of the muscle range is equally worked" (Men's Health, 2021). This comprehensive muscle engagement is key to developing both muscle strength and size.

One of the main benefits of Twenty-Ones is their impact on muscle endurance and hypertrophy. The high-rep nature of the exercise combined with the varied range of motion creates a significant metabolic stress on the muscles, which is a crucial factor in muscle growth. "The high-rep, varied-range approach of Twenty-Ones significantly enhances metabolic stress on muscles, a key factor in promoting muscle hypertrophy" (Muscle & Fitness, 2020). This metabolic stress leads to an increase in muscle size and endurance over time.

However, due to their intensity, Twenty-Ones should be used judiciously within a workout regimen. Overuse of this technique can lead to excessive muscle fatigue and potential overtraining. It's recommended to incorporate Twenty-Ones sparingly, perhaps as a finishing move in a workout session. "While Twenty-Ones are highly effective, they should be used sparingly to avoid excessive muscle fatigue" (Bodybuilding.com, 2018). This careful integration ensures that the muscles are challenged without being overwhelmed.

In summary, Twenty-Ones offer a unique and effective way to stimulate muscle growth through varied range of motion exercises. By dividing a set into three distinct parts, this technique ensures comprehensive muscle engagement, leading to improved muscle endurance and hypertrophy. The key to their effectiveness lies in the combination of high-rep stress and the targeting of different muscle fibers throughout the range of motion. However, like any intensive exercise technique, they must be integrated thoughtfully into a workout program to maximize benefits while minimizing the risk of overtraining.

Timed Sets/Reps

Timed sets/reps, a method where each repetition is performed over a specific duration, emphasize control and timing in muscle development. This approach diverges from traditional lifting by focusing not on the amount of weight lifted but on the time the muscles spend under tension. "Performing movements over a fixed duration places a different kind of stress on muscles, which can lead to increased muscle development" (Journal of Applied Physiology, 2019). The technique usually involves a slow, controlled movement during both the concentric (lifting) and eccentric (lowering) phases, typically spanning a set time like five seconds up and five seconds down.

This method's effectiveness lies in its ability to maintain constant tension on the muscle, a critical factor for muscle growth. By slowing down the movements, muscles spend more time under load, which can increase muscle fiber recruitment and metabolic stress, leading to growth. "Longer time under tension during timed sets can enhance muscle fiber recruitment, a key factor for muscle hypertrophy" (Journal of Strength and Conditioning Research, 2018). This increased time under tension makes timed sets/reps particularly useful for those looking to improve muscle endurance and achieve hypertrophy.

However, the intensity and demand of timed sets/reps necessitate careful weight selection. Using too heavy a weight can lead to form breakdown, while too light a weight might not provide sufficient stimulus for growth. "Selecting the appropriate weight is crucial in timed sets to ensure the muscles are adequately challenged without compromising form" (Strength and Conditioning Journal, 2020). This balance is vital for maximizing the benefits of the technique while minimizing the risk of injury.

Timed sets/reps also require a significant amount of mental focus and discipline. Maintaining a consistent pace throughout a set demands concentration and resilience, especially as muscle fatigue sets in. "Mental focus and discipline are as important as physical strength in timed sets, as maintaining a consistent pace is challenging" (Muscle & Fitness, 2021). This mental aspect is often what makes timed sets/reps both challenging and rewarding.

In conclusion, timed sets/reps offer a unique approach to muscle development, focusing on controlled movements and the timing of muscle contractions. By emphasizing time under tension rather than the amount of weight lifted, this technique provides a novel stimulus for muscle growth, particularly useful for improving muscle endurance and achieving muscle hypertrophy. However, its effectiveness hinges on appropriate weight selection and mental discipline to maintain a consistent pace throughout the exercise.

Partial Reps

Partial reps, a strength training technique, focus on performing movements within a limited range of motion, often used to overcome strength plateaus or target specific muscle areas. This method involves repeating an exercise movement, but only through a partial range of motion rather than the full extent. "Partial reps are effective for targeting specific muscle groups and can help overcome plateaus in strength training by focusing on the strongest part of the lift" (Journal of Strength and Conditioning Research, 2018). By isolating a portion of the movement, partial reps can intensify the stress and focus on the muscle, leading to increased muscle activation and growth in that specific area.

This technique is particularly beneficial when used at the point of an exercise where the muscle is strongest. For example, in the bench press, lifting the barbell only the top half of the range can target and strengthen the triceps and shoulders. "Utilizing partial reps at the strongest range of a movement can lead to greater strength and muscle gains in that specific area" (Muscle & Fitness, 2019). This focused approach can lead to significant improvements in overall lift strength and performance.

However, the effectiveness of partial reps depends on correct implementation and should not replace full-range exercises entirely. They are best used in conjunction with full-range movements for a well-rounded strength training program. "While partial reps can provide specific muscle benefits, they should be used as a supplement to full-range movements for balanced muscular development" (Men's Health, 2020). This balanced approach ensures comprehensive muscle growth and development.

The risk of overuse injuries should be considered when incorporating partial reps into a workout regimen. Due to the high intensity and stress placed on a specific muscle area, there is an increased risk of strain or injury. "Care should be taken when incorporating partial reps into a workout routine, as the focused intensity on a specific muscle area can lead to a higher risk of overuse injuries" (Bodybuilding.com, 2017). Proper form, weight selection, and adequate recovery are essential to minimize this risk.

In summary, partial reps offer a focused method of stimulating muscle growth and overcoming strength plateaus by isolating specific portions of an exercise's range of motion. They are particularly effective for targeting and strengthening specific muscle areas. However, for balanced muscular development and to avoid the risk of overuse injuries, partial reps should be used in moderation and in conjunction with full-range exercises.

Pre-Exhaustion

Pre-exhaustion is a technique in bodybuilding where an isolation exercise is performed before a compound movement to fatigue a targeted muscle group. This approach ensures that the specific muscle reaches a higher level of fatigue during the subsequent compound exercise. "Pre-exhaustion is used to better target a specific muscle group during compound exercises by fatiguing it with an isolation exercise first" (Journal of Strength and Conditioning Research, 2018). For instance, doing leg extensions to fatigue the quadriceps before performing squats ensures that the quads are thoroughly worked during the squat, even if other muscles involved in the squat are not as fatigued.

This technique is particularly useful when trying to overcome muscle imbalances or to further stimulate muscle growth in a specific area. By pre-exhausting a muscle, bodybuilders can ensure that the targeted muscle group reaches failure during the compound exercise, irrespective of the other, fresher muscles involved. "Pre-exhaustion allows for greater muscle fiber activation of a specific muscle group during compound lifts" (Muscle & Fitness, 2019). It's a strategic way to intensify the workout for a particular muscle, leading to potentially greater gains in size and strength for that muscle group.

However, the technique must be used carefully to avoid excessive fatigue, which could lead to a decrease in performance during the compound exercises or increase the risk of injury. The key is to fatigue the muscle, not to annihilate it before the compound movement. "The goal of pre-exhaustion is to fatigue the muscle, not to completely deplete it before the main compound exercise" (Men's Health, 2020). This approach ensures that the muscle is adequately challenged without compromising the overall workout quality or increasing the risk of injury.

Incorporating pre-exhaustion into a training program requires careful planning and attention to the body's response. It is not suitable for every workout and should be used selectively based on training goals and the body's recovery ability. "Selective use of pre-exhaustion, based on training goals and recovery, is crucial for its effectiveness" (Bodybuilding.com, 2018). Listening to the body and adjusting the intensity of the pre-exhaustion and the subsequent compound exercises is essential for maximizing the benefits of this technique.

Post-Exhaustion Sets

Post-exhaustion sets combine the use of heavy and light weights within a single exercise sequence to intensively train muscle groups. This method typically involves performing a set with heavy weights for fewer repetitions, immediately followed by a set with lighter weights for higher repetitions. "Post-exhaustion sets are effective in stimulating both types of muscle hypertrophy - myofibrillar through heavy sets and sarcoplasmic through lighter, higher-rep sets" (Journal of Strength and Conditioning Research, 2018). This combination allows bodybuilders to target both strength and muscle size within the same exercise, making it a time-efficient and comprehensive muscle-building technique.

The effectiveness of post-exhaustion sets lies in their ability to exhaust the muscle through different stimulus types. The heavy sets focus on maximal strength and muscle fiber recruitment, while the lighter sets target muscular endurance and metabolic stress. "By combining heavy and light sets, post-exhaustion training effectively fatigues the muscle through different pathways, potentially leading to greater overall muscle growth" (Men's Health, 2019). This dual approach ensures that muscles are thoroughly worked, enhancing growth and strength gains.

However, the intensity of post-exhaustion sets requires careful attention to muscle recovery and overall training volume. Due to the significant stress placed on muscles, ensuring adequate rest and nutrition is crucial for recovery and growth. "Adequate recovery strategies are essential when employing post-exhaustion sets due to the high level of muscle stress involved" (International Journal of Sports Nutrition and Exercise Metabolism, 2020). Overuse of this technique without proper recovery can lead to overtraining and hinder muscle growth.

Implementing post-exhaustion sets into a workout regimen should be done with consideration of one's overall training plan and goals. It's a technique well-suited for intermediate to advanced bodybuilders looking to intensify their workouts and challenge their muscles in new ways. "Post-exhaustion sets are most effective when strategically implemented into a well-rounded training program, especially for those seeking to overcome plateaus in muscle growth" (Bodybuilding.com, 2018). This careful integration ensures maximum benefit while minimizing the risk of injury or overtraining.

Pyramiding

Pyramiding is a versatile bodybuilding technique involving progressive adjustments in weight (load), repetitions, or rest intervals within consecutive sets of an exercise. In load pyramiding, weight increases with each set while the number of repetitions typically decreases, intensifying the challenge for the muscles. "Load pyramiding allows for a gradual increase in weight, effectively warming up the muscles in the initial sets and maximizing strength in the latter sets" (Journal of Strength and Conditioning Research, 2019). This method is particularly effective for building strength, as it allows for heavy lifting when the muscles are thoroughly warmed up.

Repetition pyramiding, on the other hand, involves altering the number of repetitions per set, either increasing or decreasing across the sets. This can either start with high reps and low weight, gradually moving to low reps and high weight, or vice versa. "Repetition pyramiding challenges the muscles by varying the volume and intensity within a workout, which can lead to increased muscle endurance and hypertrophy" (Men's Health, 2020). This variation in volume and intensity can stimulate muscle growth in different ways compared to a standard set structure.

Rest pyramiding adjusts the rest intervals between sets, usually starting with shorter rest periods and increasing them with each set, or the reverse. This technique manipulates the recovery time of the muscles, impacting the intensity of the workout. "Adjusting rest intervals in a pyramiding manner can significantly influence the intensity and focus of a workout, affecting both strength and endurance" (Muscle & Fitness, 2021). By manipulating rest periods, bodybuilders can target different aspects of muscle performance.

Incorporating pyramiding techniques into a training program requires careful planning and an understanding of one's training goals. Whether focusing on load, repetitions, or rest, each method of pyramiding offers a unique way to challenge the muscles, leading to different training adaptations. "Strategic use of different pyramiding techniques can optimize a training program to meet specific strength, size, or endurance goals" (Bodybuilding.com, 2018). This customization is what makes pyramiding a popular and effective approach in strength training and bodybuilding.

Advanced Training Techniques

Load Pyramiding and Load Sets

Load pyramiding and load sets are key techniques in advanced strength training, focusing on progressively increasing the weight while varying the number of repetitions. Load pyramiding typically involves starting with lighter weights and higher repetitions, gradually increasing the weight and decreasing the repetitions across successive sets. This method not only warms up the muscles effectively but also prepares them for the heavier loads to come, maximizing strength and hypertrophy gains. "Load pyramiding is an effective way to progressively overload the muscles, leading to significant increases in strength and muscle size" (Journal of Strength and Conditioning Research, 2019). Load sets, on the other hand, involve increasing the weight within a single set, often immediately after a set number of repetitions. This approach intensifies the stress on the muscles within the same set, challenging them further and promoting muscle growth. "Incorporating load sets within a workout can significantly increase muscle stimulation, as it combines volume and intensity in a single set" (Strength and Conditioning Journal, 2020). Both techniques are designed to push the muscles beyond their comfort zone, promoting adaptation and growth.

Break-downs

Break-downs are an advanced bodybuilding technique designed to intensify workouts by reducing weights immediately after reaching muscle failure. This method involves performing an exercise until no more repetitions are possible, then quickly lowering the weight and continuing to do more repetitions until failure is reached again. "Break downs extend a set past the point of initial muscle failure, allowing for deeper muscle fiber recruitment and enhanced muscle fatigue, which are key drivers for muscle hypertrophy" (Journal of Strength and Conditioning Research, 2020). By pushing the muscles beyond their usual limits, break downs create a highly intense environment that can lead to increased muscle growth and endurance. This technique is particularly effective for experienced lifters seeking to overcome plateaus and enhance their muscle gains. However, due to its intensity, break downs should be used cautiously to avoid overtraining and ensure adequate muscle recovery.

Pre-exhaustion with Break-downs

Combining pre-exhaustion with break-downs is an advanced bodybuilding strategy that maximizes muscle growth by integrating two intense techniques. Pre-exhaustion involves performing an isolation exercise to target a specific muscle group before a compound movement, ensuring the targeted muscle reaches fatigue early in the compound exercise. "Pre-exhaustion effectively fatigues a muscle group before a compound exercise, ensuring it is fully activated throughout the workout" (Journal of Strength and Conditioning Research, 2019). Break-downs, performed after reaching muscle failure, involve immediately reducing the weight and continuing with more repetitions. This combination is powerful: pre-exhaustion ensures the muscle group is already fatigued when starting the compound exercise, and break-downs push these muscles beyond their normal failure point. "The combination of pre-exhaustion and break-downs can lead to heightened muscle activation and superior hypertrophy, compared to using these techniques in isolation" (Strength and Conditioning Journal, 2021). This approach requires careful monitoring to avoid overtraining and ensure adequate recovery, given its high intensity.

Workout Schedules and Routines

Creating an effective workout schedule is essential for optimal muscle development and overall fitness. A well-planned routine targets different muscle groups on specific days, allowing for focused training and adequate recovery time. For instance, a common weekly layout might designate Monday for chest exercises, such as bench presses and push-ups, ensuring a powerful start to the week. Tuesday could then shift focus to back muscles with exercises like rows and lat pull-downs, allowing the chest muscles to recover while engaging a different set of muscles. Midweek, attention could turn to the lower body, with Wednesday dedicated to leg workouts, including squats, lunges, and leg presses, providing a comprehensive lower body routine.

Continuing through the week, Thursday might focus on shoulders, incorporating movements like overhead presses and lateral raises to target all aspects of the deltoids. On Friday, the routine could shift to arms, with bicep curls and tricep extensions, ensuring these smaller muscle groups receive dedicated attention. The weekend can then offer a change of pace: Saturday might include a lighter, full-body workout or cardio session, promoting active recovery and cardiovascular health, while Sunday could be reserved for complete rest or light activities like walking or yoga, allowing the body to recover and prepare for the upcoming week.

This schedule is just a template and should be adjusted based on individual needs and goals. For someone focusing on building size and strength, incorporating heavy weights with lower repetitions would be key, while someone aiming for endurance and toning might focus on higher repetitions with lighter weights. Each workout session should last around 45 to 60 minutes, striking a balance between intensity and overtraining.

In addition to this weekly structure, it's vital to periodically change the routine. Varying exercises, order, intensity, and volume can prevent plateaus, a state where the body adapts to the workout, slowing progress. "Muscle confusion, or changing your workout routine regularly, can help maximize muscle growth and prevent plateaus" (Bodybuilding.com, 2021). This variation can be as simple as substituting barbells for dumbbells, altering the grip or angle of an exercise, or incorporating completely new exercises.

The intensity of each workout should be balanced with adequate rest and nutrition. Each muscle group needs time to recover and grow after being exercised, typically requiring 48 to 72 hours. Hence, organizing the workout schedule to avoid training the same muscle group on consecutive days is crucial. "Giving each muscle group adequate time to recover is as important as the workout itself for muscle growth" (Journal of Exercise Science & Fitness, 2020). Adequate protein intake and hydration, alongside quality sleep, are also integral to support muscle recovery and growth.

Tailoring the routine to personal goals, experience level, and physical condition is essential. Beginners might start with lighter weights and basic compound movements, gradually increasing intensity as their strength and endurance improve. More experienced lifters might incorporate advanced techniques like supersets, dropsets, or pyramiding to further challenge their muscles.

"Personalizing your workout routine is key to achieving your fitness goals and prevents the risk of injury" (Men's Health, 2021). This personalization ensures the workout remains challenging yet achievable, minimizing the risk of injury and maximizing the potential for muscle growth and fitness improvements.

Overall, the key to a successful workout schedule is balance – balancing different muscle groups, balancing intensity with rest, and balancing personal goals with effective training strategies. A well-planned workout schedule, when combined with proper nutrition and rest, can lead to significant improvements in muscle size, strength, and overall fitness.

Personalizing Your Workout

Personalizing your workout is crucial for effectiveness and safety, catering to individual fitness levels, goals, and body responses. For beginners, it's essential to start with basic exercises that build foundational strength and endurance. Starting with lighter weights and focusing on form can prevent injuries and build a solid base. "Beginners should focus on mastering form with lighter weights before progressing to heavier loads" (American Council on Exercise, 2020). Initially, full-body workouts two to three times a week can help acclimate the body to strength training. As strength and comfort with the exercises increase, the workout can be gradually intensified by increasing weights, adding more sets, or incorporating more challenging exercises.

For intermediate lifters, the focus shifts to more specialized routines that target specific muscle groups. This can involve splitting workouts into upper and lower body days, or isolating specific muscle groups each day. Intermediate lifters can start experimenting with different types of equipment and techniques, such as dumbbells, barbells, and resistance machines. "Intermediate lifters should begin to incorporate a variety of equipment and techniques to challenge their muscles in different ways" (Journal of Strength and Conditioning Research, 2019). This is also a stage where lifters can start to introduce techniques like supersets or drop sets to intensify their workouts.

Advanced bodybuilders require a more strategic approach, often focusing on very specific muscle development and strength goals. Their routines might involve a high degree of specialization with advanced techniques like pyramiding, pre-exhaustion, and periodization. "Advanced bodybuilders should employ a range of specialized techniques to continue challenging their muscles and avoid plateaus" (Muscle & Fitness, 2021). Advanced lifters also need to be particularly mindful of their body's response to training, carefully balancing intensity, volume, and recovery to optimize growth and prevent injury.

Regardless of the level, rest and recovery are vital components of any training regimen. Muscles need time to repair and grow after a workout. Overtraining can lead to fatigue, decreased performance, and increased risk of injury. "Adequate rest and recovery are as important as the workout itself, allowing for muscle repair and growth" (Journal of Sports Sciences, 2018). This includes not only rest days but also ensuring adequate sleep and proper nutrition, particularly sufficient protein intake for muscle repair.

Incorporating variety in workouts is important to keep the body guessing and muscles adapting. Changing up the routine every few weeks can prevent boredom and plateauing. This could mean altering the exercises, adjusting the number of repetitions and sets, or changing the order of the workout. "Regularly changing your workout routine is essential for continuous improvement and to keep the workouts engaging" (Bodybuilding.com, 2020).

Personalizing a workout also means listening to your body and adjusting the workout accordingly. This might involve reducing intensity if feeling fatigued or stepping up the workout if it feels too easy. Being in tune with your body helps in customizing the workout to meet individual needs effectively. "Listening to your body and adjusting your workout accordingly is key for effective and safe training" (Men's Health, 2021).

Workout Splits Introduction

Workout splits are systematic approaches to dividing physical training across different days, focusing on specific muscle groups or types of exercise in each session. This methodical separation allows for targeted muscle engagement and recovery, a critical aspect in building strength, endurance, and overall fitness. Understanding workout splits is crucial for anyone serious about their fitness routine, whether a beginner or an experienced athlete. The right split can significantly enhance training results by optimizing muscle recovery, preventing overtraining, and ensuring a balanced workout regimen.

The first step in understanding workout splits is recognizing their fundamental purpose: to allocate specific days to work on different muscle groups or fitness aspects. For instance, a typical split might designate separate days for upper body, lower body, and cardiovascular training. This separation is not a mere whim of fitness enthusiasts but is rooted in the science of muscle recovery and growth. When a muscle group is intensely worked out, it needs time to repair and strengthen. Without adequate rest, muscles cannot recover fully, leading to a plateau or even a decline in performance and an increased risk of injury. Workout splits respect this physiological need by providing rest periods for each muscle group while allowing other parts of the body to be trained.

Another critical aspect of workout splits is their adaptability. They can be tailored to individual needs, goals, and schedules. For instance, a three-day split might work for someone with limited time, focusing on full-body workouts each session. In contrast, a five or six-day split could allow more dedicated focus on each muscle group, ideal for those aiming for hypertrophy or specialized athletic training. The flexibility of workout splits means they can be adjusted as goals or circumstances change, making them a sustainable approach to fitness.

Selecting the right workout split requires an understanding of one's own goals and physical condition. A beginner might benefit from a full-body workout split, where each session involves exercises targeting all major muscle groups. This approach promotes overall muscular balance and strength, a foundation upon which more specialized training can be built. On the other hand, someone with specific goals, like building muscle mass or improving athletic performance, might opt for a split that allows for more focused and intense training on specific muscle groups.

Experience level plays a significant role in choosing a workout split. Beginners often respond well to full-body routines as their bodies are not yet accustomed to high-intensity or high-volume training. As one progresses, the body adapts and may require more targeted stimuli for further improvement. This adaptation is where more advanced splits, such as upper/lower or push/pull/legs, come into play. These splits allow for more intense sessions with a higher volume of exercises for each muscle group, necessitating a longer recovery period for each.

While workout splits are predominantly about training, they cannot be separated from the context of overall fitness, which includes nutrition, rest, and lifestyle factors. Proper nutrition provides the energy and building blocks needed for exercise and recovery. A diet lacking in essential nutrients or energy can undermine the effectiveness of even the most well-planned workout split. Similarly, rest and sleep are not just times of inactivity but critical periods when the body repairs and strengthens itself. Neglecting rest can lead to overtraining, fatigue, and a decrease in performance.

It's also essential to be aware of the common mistakes people make with workout splits. One of the most frequent errors is not allowing adequate recovery time, leading to overtraining and potential injuries. Another mistake is focusing too much on preferred exercises or muscle groups, leading to imbalances and weaknesses. A well-designed workout split should provide a balanced approach to training, ensuring that all major muscle groups are worked and developed evenly.

Periodic assessment and adjustment of workout splits are necessary. As the body adapts to a specific training routine, it may require new challenges to continue progressing. This adaptation is why it's advisable to periodically review and modify workout routines. Adjustments can include changing the exercises, increasing the intensity or volume of workouts, or even switching to a different type of split altogether.

In conclusion, workout splits are powerful tools in the arsenal of fitness training. They offer a structured approach to exercise, ensuring balanced training, adequate recovery, and continual progression. Whether you are just starting your fitness journey or looking to optimize your training, understanding and effectively utilizing workout splits can significantly enhance your results. This chapter has provided the foundational knowledge needed to comprehend and apply these principles, empowering you to take control of your fitness regimen with confidence and clarity.

The Essence of Workout Splits

Workout splits represent a strategic division of exercise routines, crucial for achieving specific fitness goals. They are not mere scheduling conveniences but a deliberate method to enhance training effectiveness and efficiency. At their core, workout splits involve dividing exercise routines across different days to focus on specific muscle groups or types of exercise each session. This methodical approach allows for targeted muscle engagement and adequate recovery, vital in building strength, endurance, and overall fitness. Understanding workout splits is essential for anyone serious about their fitness regimen, whether they are a novice or an experienced athlete.

The primary purpose of workout splits is to allocate specific days to work on different muscle groups or fitness aspects. For example, a typical split might designate separate days for upper body, lower body, and cardiovascular training. This separation aligns with the science of muscle recovery and growth. Intense workouts require muscles to repair and strengthen, necessitating time for recovery. Without adequate rest, muscles cannot recover fully, leading to a plateau or decline in performance and an increased risk of injury. Workout splits respect this physiological need by providing rest periods for each muscle group while allowing other parts of the body to be trained.

Adaptability is a key feature of workout splits. They can be tailored to individual needs, goals, and schedules. A three-day split might work for someone with limited time, focusing on full-body workouts each session. In contrast, a five or six-day split could allow more dedicated focus on each muscle group, ideal for those aiming for hypertrophy or specialized athletic training. The flexibility of workout splits means they can be adjusted as goals or circumstances change, making them a sustainable approach to fitness.

Selecting the right workout split requires an understanding of one's own goals and physical condition. A beginner might benefit from a full-body workout split, where each session involves exercises targeting all major muscle groups. This approach promotes overall muscular balance and strength, a foundation upon which more specialized training can be built. Conversely, someone with specific goals, like building muscle mass or improving athletic performance, might opt for a split that allows for more focused and intense training on specific muscle groups.

Experience level plays a significant role in choosing a workout split. Beginners often respond well to full-body routines as their bodies are not yet accustomed to high-intensity or high-volume training. As one progresses, the body adapts and may require more targeted stimuli for further improvement. This adaptation is where more advanced splits, such as upper/lower or push/pull/legs, come into play. These splits allow for more intense sessions with a higher volume of exercises for each muscle group, necessitating a longer recovery period for each.

While workout splits are predominantly about training, they cannot be separated from the context of overall fitness, which includes nutrition, rest, and lifestyle factors. Proper nutrition provides the energy and building blocks needed for exercise and recovery. A diet lacking in essential nutrients or energy can undermine the effectiveness of even the most well-planned workout split. Similarly, rest and sleep are not just times of inactivity but critical periods when the body repairs and strengthens itself. Neglecting rest can lead to overtraining, fatigue, and a decrease in performance.

It's also essential to be aware of the common mistakes people make with workout splits. One of the most frequent errors is not allowing adequate recovery time, leading to overtraining and potential injuries. Another mistake is focusing too much on preferred exercises or muscle groups, leading to imbalances and weaknesses. A well-designed workout split should provide a balanced approach to training, ensuring that all major muscle groups are worked and developed evenly.

Periodic assessment and adjustment of workout splits are necessary. As the body adapts to a specific training routine, it may require new challenges to continue progressing. This adaptation is why it's advisable to periodically review and modify workout routines. Adjustments can include changing the exercises, increasing the intensity or volume of workouts, or even switching to a different type of split altogether.

In conclusion, workout splits are powerful tools in the arsenal of fitness training. They offer a structured approach to exercise, ensuring balanced training, adequate recovery, and continual progression. Whether you are just starting your fitness journey or looking to optimize your training, understanding and effectively utilizing workout splits can significantly enhance your results. This chapter has provided the foundational knowledge needed to comprehend and apply these principles, empowering you to take control of your fitness regimen with confidence and clarity.

The Science Behind Splitting Workouts

Workout splits are integral to effective fitness regimes, allowing for optimized muscle recovery, minimized risk of overtraining, and enhanced muscle growth. The science behind these benefits is rooted in understanding how the human body responds to stress, particularly the stress of exercise. When muscles are subjected to the strain of weight lifting or intense physical activity, they experience microscopic tears. This damage, while sounding negative, is the catalyst for muscle growth and strength increase. During the recovery period, the body repairs these tears, and in doing so, the muscles grow stronger and larger. However, this process requires time and the right conditions, including adequate rest and proper nutrition.

The principle of recovery is where workout splits play a crucial role. By dividing the training schedule into segments that focus on different muscle groups, workout splits allow certain areas of the body to rest and recover while others are being worked. For example, an upper/lower split allows the upper body muscles to rest while the lower body is trained, and vice versa. This approach not only prevents overworking any single muscle group but also ensures that each has the maximum amount of time to recover before being stressed again.

Optimized recovery is essential not just for muscle growth but also for avoiding overtraining syndrome. Overtraining occurs when there's an imbalance between training and recovery, where the body does not have sufficient time to recuperate between workouts. Symptoms of overtraining include prolonged fatigue, decreased performance, and even injury. By utilizing workout splits, the risk of overtraining is significantly reduced as each muscle group is given ample time to recover.

Workout splits also contribute to increased muscle hypertrophy, which is the enlargement of muscle cells. When a muscle group is targeted with sufficient intensity during a workout, it triggers the body's anabolic processes, which repair and build muscle tissue. This process is most efficient when the muscle group is allowed to fully recover before being worked again. Different types of workout splits cater to different training goals and intensities, enabling individuals to tailor their training according to their specific hypertrophy goals.

In addition to muscle recovery and growth, workout splits also aid in better workout planning and execution. By having a structured plan that clearly defines which muscle groups to work on and when it allows for more focused and effective workouts. This structure ensures that all major muscle groups are worked evenly over time, promoting balanced muscular development and reducing the likelihood of muscle imbalances.

Nutrition plays a complementary role in the effectiveness of workout splits. Adequate protein intake is crucial for muscle repair and growth, while carbohydrates provide the energy needed for intense workouts. Ensuring a balanced intake of macronutrients, vitamins, and minerals supports the body's recovery processes and overall health, which in turn maximizes the benefits gained from workout splits.

Flexibility in workout splits is another key factor in their effectiveness. Individuals can adjust the frequency, intensity, and volume of workouts in their split to match their personal fitness level, goals, and schedule. This flexibility allows for progressive overload, where the intensity of workouts is gradually increased to challenge the muscles continuously and promote further growth and strength gains.

Workout splits also have a psychological benefit, providing a clear and structured approach to training that can boost motivation and focus. Knowing exactly what to train on a given day reduces decision fatigue and increases adherence to a fitness regimen. This structured approach also makes it easier to track progress and make adjustments as needed.

Tailoring Your Split: Factors to Consider

When it comes to tailoring a workout split, several key factors must be considered to ensure the regimen is effective, sustainable, and aligned with personal goals. One of the primary considerations is the individual's experience level. Beginners often benefit from simpler workout splits. These typically involve full-body routines or compound movements that engage multiple muscle groups simultaneously. Such routines are not only efficient for those new to exercising but also provide a solid foundation for overall fitness and muscle development. As individuals become more experienced and their bodies adapt to regular training, they may require more specialized splits. Advanced athletes or those with specific strength or bodybuilding goals might opt for splits that isolate muscle groups, allowing for more focused and intense training on each area.

Fitness goals are another critical factor in determining the right workout split. For strength building, splits that allow for heavy lifting with ample recovery time for each muscle group are ideal. These often involve working different muscle groups on different days, such as an upper/lower split or a push/pull/legs split. For endurance enhancement, a mix of cardiovascular training and strength training might be necessary, with more frequent but less intense workouts. Those aiming for fat loss might benefit from a combination of strength training and high-intensity interval training (HIIT) to maximize calorie burn.

Time availability is a practical consideration that significantly influences the choice of workout split. The amount of time one can dedicate to working out each week will determine the feasibility and effectiveness of different splits. Individuals with limited time may opt for full-body workouts that can be done two or three times a week. In contrast, those with more time available might choose a split that allows for daily training, focusing on different muscle groups each day for more detailed muscle sculpting and strength gains.

Individual recovery rates are crucial in dictating the intensity and frequency of workouts. Recovery is when muscles repair and grow stronger, and it varies from person to person. Some individuals may recover quickly and be able to handle high-frequency training, while others might need longer recovery periods to avoid overtraining and injury. Listening to the body and adjusting the workout split accordingly is essential for long-term progress and health.

Finally, equipment access also plays a role in determining the type of exercises included in a workout split. Those with access to a fully equipped gym have a wider range of exercises to choose from, allowing for more variety and specificity in their training. However, individuals working out at home with limited equipment can still achieve effective workouts by focusing on bodyweight exercises, dumbbells, or resistance bands. The key is to choose a split and exercises that align with the available resources while still challenging the body and progressing toward fitness goals.

Tailoring a workout split requires careful consideration of several factors, including experience level, fitness goals, time availability, individual recovery rates, and equipment access. By addressing these factors, individuals can design a workout split that is not only effective in helping them reach their fitness goals but also enjoyable and sustainable in the long run. The right workout split is a powerful tool in any fitness journey, providing structure and direction while accommodating individual needs and circumstances.

A Balanced Approach: Combining Science with Individual Needs

The effectiveness of workout splits hinges on a crucial balance between scientific principles and individual needs. This balance is what makes a workout split not just a regimen, but a personalized fitness plan that aligns with specific goals, preferences, and lifestyle. The foundational aspects of workout splits are rooted in exercise science, focusing on how the body responds to different types of training stimuli. By understanding these principles, one can create a workout split that maximizes muscle growth, strength gains, and overall fitness.

One of the key scientific principles underlying workout splits is the concept of muscle hypertrophy, which involves increasing muscle size through resistance training. To achieve hypertrophy, muscles must be subjected to a level of stress that challenges them beyond their current capacity. This is where the design of workout splits comes into play. By dividing training into sessions that focus on different muscle groups, individuals can apply the necessary stress to each muscle group while allowing others to recover. This approach not only maximizes muscle growth but also minimizes the risk of overtraining and injury.

Another scientific aspect critical to workout splits is the principle of progressive overload. This involves gradually increasing the weight, frequency, or intensity of workouts to continuously challenge the muscles. A well-designed workout split should incorporate this principle, allowing for consistent progress over time. Whether it's adding more weight to the barbell or increasing the number of reps and sets, progressive overload is a fundamental element of successful workout regimens.

While these scientific principles are essential, the effectiveness of a workout split also heavily depends on personal factors. Individual fitness goals play a significant role in shaping the structure of a workout split. For example, someone aiming for general fitness might prefer a full-body workout split that provides a balanced approach to muscle development. In contrast, an individual focused on bodybuilding might opt for a split that isolates specific muscle groups, allowing for more targeted and intense training.

Personal preferences and lifestyle are also crucial in determining the right workout split. Factors like schedule constraints, workout enjoyment, and motivation levels need to be considered. A workout split that aligns with an individual's daily routine and personal preferences is more likely to be sustainable and enjoyable. For instance, someone with a busy schedule might find a three-day full-body workout more manageable than a six-day split.

Recovery capabilities are another personal factor that must be taken into account. Recovery is a critical component of fitness, as muscles grow and repair during rest periods. Individuals need to consider their own recovery rates when designing a workout split. Some may recover quickly and be able to handle frequent and intense workouts, while others may require more rest days to avoid fatigue and overtraining.

Finally, equipment availability can influence the choice of exercises in a workout split. Those with access to a well-equipped gym can incorporate a wide range of exercises in their routine, from machine-based workouts to free weights. However, those working out at home with limited equipment can still have effective workouts by focusing on bodyweight exercises and using whatever equipment they have available.

The Full Body Split

The full body split is a foundational approach to strength training and overall fitness. This regimen entails targeting all major muscle groups within a single workout session, and is typically executed two to three times a week. Such a frequency ensures that each muscle group receives adequate attention while allowing substantial recovery time between sessions. This split is particularly beneficial for muscle growth and overall fitness improvement, making it an excellent choice for both beginners and seasoned athletes.

For beginners, the full body split serves as an introduction to strength training, covering all bases in a few sessions per week. It provides a holistic approach, ensuring that no major muscle group is neglected. This split is beneficial for building a strong foundation of muscle strength and endurance, which is crucial for more advanced training. Moreover, it's an efficient way to exercise, especially for those with limited time, as it offers a comprehensive workout in a single session.

Experienced athletes also find value in the full body split. It can be used as a method of maintaining muscle mass and strength, or as a way to break through plateaus by changing the routine. This split allows for a high degree of flexibility in terms of exercise selection, intensity, and volume. Advanced lifters can incorporate a range of exercises, from compound movements like squats, deadlifts, and bench presses, to isolation exercises targeting specific muscle groups.

One of the key advantages of the full body split is the balanced development it promotes. By engaging all major muscle groups in a single session, it ensures that no part of the body is over or under-trained. This balance is crucial not only for aesthetic purposes but also for functional strength and injury prevention. A well-rounded physique is less prone to injuries and better equipped to handle various physical challenges.

Recovery is another significant aspect of the full body split. Since this routine is typically spread out over two to three days a week, it allows muscles adequate time to recover and grow. Recovery is a critical part of the muscle-building process; without it, muscles cannot repair the micro-tears that occur during strength training. This split provides the perfect balance between training and rest, making it ideal for sustained muscle growth.

The full body split also offers versatility in terms of intensity and volume. Depending on individual fitness goals and preferences, one can adjust the number of exercises, sets, and reps for each muscle group. Beginners might start with fewer exercises and lower volume, gradually increasing as they become more comfortable and their fitness improves. On the other hand, more advanced athletes might focus on increasing the intensity of their workouts, either by adding more weight, incorporating advanced techniques like supersets and drop sets, or reducing rest periods between sets.

Another benefit of the full body split is its effectiveness for fat loss. By engaging multiple large muscle groups in a single session, it creates a high metabolic demand, burning a significant number of calories both during and after the workout. This makes it an efficient tool for those looking to lose weight while maintaining or building muscle mass.

Balanced muscle development is a cornerstone of the full body split. Each session targets every major muscle group, ensuring a harmonious development of the entire body. This holistic approach prevents the common issue of muscle imbalances that can occur with more specialized splits. For instance, focusing excessively on the upper body while neglecting the lower body can lead to disproportion and potentially increase the risk of injuries. The full body split circumvents this by providing a balanced workout routine, promoting symmetrical muscle growth and functional strength.

Flexibility is another significant benefit. The full body split can be easily adapted to various schedules and fitness levels, making it a practical choice for a broad range of individuals. Whether one is a busy professional with limited time for the gym, a stay-at-home parent juggling numerous responsibilities, or someone who travels frequently, this split can be tailored to fit into almost any lifestyle. The workouts can be compressed or extended based on time constraints and personal preferences, making it a highly adaptable training approach.

Efficiency is a key attribute of the full body split, particularly appealing to those with limited time. Each session delivers a complete workout, engaging all major muscle groups. This means that even if an individual can only spare a few days a week for exercise, they can still achieve comprehensive fitness results. This efficiency makes the full body split an excellent choice for people who want to maximize their workout time.

Recovery-friendly nature of the full body split is crucial for muscle repair and growth. Ample rest between sessions is provided, allowing each muscle group to recover fully before being worked again. This rest period is essential for the repair of muscle fibers that break down during exercise, a process that leads to muscle growth and strength gains. Adequate recovery also reduces the risk of overtraining and injuries, making the full body split a sustainable and safe workout regimen.

The variety offered in the full body split keeps workouts engaging and challenging. Unlike routines that repetitively focus on the same muscle groups, the full body split allows for a wide range of exercises targeting different areas of the body. This variety not only prevents boredom but also challenges muscles in diverse ways, contributing to better overall fitness and preventing plateauing.

Sample full body workout routines demonstrate the adaptability of this split to different fitness levels. Beginners can focus on compound movements like squats, bench presses, deadlifts, and overhead presses, interspersed with bodyweight exercises like push-ups and planks. These foundational exercises build overall strength and muscle endurance, providing a solid base for more advanced training.

For intermediate fitness enthusiasts, incorporating more variety in the routine is beneficial. This can include exercises like lunges, pull-ups, and dumbbell rows, which build on the foundation set by the basic compound movements. These exercises introduce new challenges and help continue the development of strength and muscle mass.

Advanced routines can add complexity with plyometric exercises, supersets, and higher intensity training techniques. These additions increase the intensity of the workouts, pushing the limits of strength, endurance, and muscular power. Advanced routines are designed to challenge even the most experienced athletes, ensuring continuous progression and development.

The full body split is ideal for various individuals, each with unique reasons for choosing this approach. Beginners find it beneficial as it offers a foundational approach to strength and fitness, covering all bases in a few sessions per week. This solid foundation is crucial for future progression in more specialized or intense training routines.

Individuals with limited time find the full body split ideal as it allows them to maintain a high level of fitness with just a few gym sessions each week. Every session is comprehensive, ensuring that despite the limited frequency, the effectiveness of their workouts is not compromised.

Those seeking balanced development, aiming for overall fitness rather than specializing in one area, benefit greatly from the full body split. It ensures that all muscle groups receive equal attention, leading to a well-rounded physique and functional strength.

Lastly, recovery-conscious individuals, including those who need or prefer more rest days due to personal preferences, lifestyle constraints, or age, find the full body split aligns well with their requirements. The built-in rest periods between workout days help in maintaining a healthy balance between exercise and recovery, crucial

Example Full Body Workout Routines

Full body workout routines can be tailored to suit various fitness levels, from beginners to advanced trainers. Each level focuses on different types of exercises and intensities to match the individual's skill and strength.

Beginner Routine

For beginners, the focus is on mastering the basic compound movements, which work multiple muscle groups simultaneously, providing a solid foundation for strength and muscle development. A typical beginner's full body routine might include:

- Squats: 3 sets of 8-10 reps. Squats are fundamental for building lower body strength and engaging core muscles.
- Bench Press: 3 sets of 8-10 reps. This exercise targets the chest, shoulders, and triceps.

- Deadlifts: 3 sets of 8-10 reps. Deadlifts are excellent for developing the back, glutes, and hamstrings.

- Overhead Press: 3 sets of 8-10 reps. This movement strengthens the shoulders and upper back.

- Push-Ups: 2 sets of 10-15 reps. Push-ups are a great bodyweight exercise for the chest, triceps, and shoulders.

- Planks: 2 sets, holding for 30 seconds to 1 minute. Planks are effective for core strengthening.

This routine should be performed two to three times a week, with at least one day of rest between sessions to allow for muscle recovery.

Intermediate Routine

Intermediate routines introduce more variety and slightly higher intensity. The addition of new exercises helps to further challenge the muscles and promote continued growth and strength gains.

- Lunges: 3 sets of 10 reps per leg. Lunges are great for targeting the quadriceps, glutes, and hamstrings.

- Pull-Ups: 3 sets of 6-8 reps. Pull-ups are effective for strengthening the upper back, biceps, and forearms.

- Dumbbell Rows: 3 sets of 8-10 reps per arm. This exercise focuses on the back muscles and biceps.

- Incline Bench Press: 3 sets of 8-10 reps. This variation targets the upper chest more than the flat bench press.

- Leg Press: 3 sets of 10 reps. Leg press machines are good for targeting the quads and glutes.

- Russian Twists: 3 sets of 15 reps per side. This exercise is great for oblique and core strength.

Intermediate routines can be done two to four times a week, depending on recovery and individual fitness goals.

Advanced Routine

Advanced routines are designed for those who have a solid fitness base and are looking to further challenge themselves. These routines often include higher intensity exercises, plyometrics, and supersets.

- Plyometric Box Jumps: 3 sets of 8-10 reps. Box jumps are excellent for developing explosive power in the legs.

- Superset: Barbell Squats and Deadlifts: 3 sets of 6-8 reps each. Performing these exercises back-to-back increases the intensity of the workout.

- Weighted Pull-Ups: 3 sets of 6-8 reps. Adding weight increases the difficulty of pull-ups.

- Dumbbell Snatch: 3 sets of 6-8 reps per arm. This is a full-body explosive movement that improves power and coordination.

- Superset: Dips and Push-Ups: 3 sets of 10-12 reps each. This combination works the chest and triceps intensely.

- Hanging Leg Raises: 3 sets of 10-15 reps. This exercise is challenging for the core, especially the lower abdominals.

Advanced routines can be performed three to five times a week, allowing for at least one day of rest between sessions for optimal muscle recovery and growth.

Each of these routines, from beginner to advanced, can be adjusted in terms of sets, reps, and weight to suit individual needs and progress. It's important to listen to the body and modify the workout as needed, ensuring consistent progression while avoiding injury.

The Upper/Lower Split

The upper/lower split is a dynamic and efficient approach to strength training and muscle building. This workout regimen involves dividing exercises into two primary categories: those that target the upper body and those that focus on the lower body. Typically, this split is structured over a four-day cycle, with two days dedicated to upper body workouts and two days for lower body workouts. The remaining days are reserved for rest or active recovery, making this split highly effective for both muscle development and recovery.

In an upper/lower split, the focus on upper body workouts involves exercises targeting the chest, back, shoulders, and arms. This concentrated effort on the upper half of the body during these sessions allows for intensive work on these muscle groups. The specific exercises might include bench presses, pull-ups, shoulder presses, and bicep curls, among others. Each of these exercises is designed to maximize muscle engagement in the upper body, contributing to improved strength and muscle definition.

The lower body days focus on the legs and glutes, involving exercises such as squats, deadlifts, lunges, and calf raises. These movements are crucial for building lower body strength and size. By dedicating entire sessions to the lower body, the split ensures that these major muscle groups receive the attention and workload necessary for growth and development.

One of the primary benefits of the upper/lower split is the focused training it offers. By concentrating on one half of the body at a time, it allows for a more intense workout session for each muscle group. This focused approach leads to better muscle fatigue and, consequently, more significant muscle growth and strength gains. It enables individuals to push their upper and lower body muscles to the limit, ensuring each workout's effectiveness.

Flexibility is another significant advantage of the upper/lower split. It can be tailored to fit various schedules and adjusted in frequency. For example, those with less time during the week can compress the split into a three-day cycle, focusing on full-body workouts. Alternatively, those who can dedicate more time can expand the split to a five or six-day cycle, allowing for more targeted exercises and increased volume.

The variety offered in the upper/lower split is crucial in preventing workout monotony. By alternating between upper and lower body workouts, individuals can incorporate a wide range of exercises, keeping the routine interesting and engaging. This variety not only maintains motivation but also ensures that all muscle groups are being worked effectively, reducing the risk of muscle imbalances.

Another critical aspect of the upper/lower split is recovery optimization. Each muscle group is given adequate time to rest and recover before being worked again. This recovery is essential for muscle repair and growth, as muscles grow during rest periods, not during the workouts themselves. By structuring the split to include rest or active recovery days, it promotes overall muscle recovery, reducing the risk of overtraining and injuries.

In conclusion, the upper/lower split is a versatile and effective approach to fitness training. Its structure allows for focused and intense workouts for both the upper and lower body, ensuring balanced muscle development and strength gains. The flexibility of the split makes it suitable for a wide range of individuals with different schedules and fitness goals. Its emphasis on recovery optimizes muscle growth and minimizes the risk of injury, making it a sustainable and effective workout regimen for anyone looking to improve their fitness.

Example Upper and Lower Body Workouts

The upper/lower split is a training method widely recognized for its efficiency in building strength and muscle mass. This approach divides workouts into two main categories: upper body and lower body routines. Each routine targets specific muscle groups, allowing for concentrated effort and optimal muscle development. Advanced techniques such as supersets, drop sets, and isolation exercises can further intensify these workouts, offering seasoned athletes a challenging and effective training regimen.

Upper Body Routine

The upper body routine primarily focuses on exercises that target the chest, back, shoulders, and arms. Key exercises in this routine include:

- Bench Presses: A fundamental exercise for developing chest strength and size. It also engages the triceps and shoulders. Performing 3-4 sets of 6-10 repetitions is ideal for muscle growth.

- Pull-Ups: Effective for working the upper back and biceps. Pull-ups also engage the core and improve overall upper body strength. Aim for 3 sets of as many reps as possible.

- Shoulder Presses: This exercise targets the deltoids and triceps. It's crucial for building shoulder strength and stability. 3 sets of 6-10 reps are recommended.

- Bicep Curls: Essential for building bicep strength and size. They also help in improving grip strength. Perform 3 sets of 8-12 reps.

These exercises should be performed with proper form and a weight that challenges the muscles while still allowing for the full range of motion. The upper body routine can be varied by including different variations of these exercises, such as incline bench presses or dumbbell curls, to target the muscles differently and avoid plateaus.

Lower Body Routine

The lower body routine focuses on exercises that target the quadriceps, hamstrings, glutes, and calves. Essential exercises for this routine include:

- Squats: A cornerstone exercise for lower body strength, targeting the quadriceps, hamstrings, and glutes. Aiming for 3-4 sets of 6-10 reps is effective for building strength and muscle.

- Deadlifts: Excellent for developing overall lower body strength, particularly in the hamstrings and glutes. Perform 3 sets of 6-8 reps.

- Lunges: Lunges are versatile and target the quadriceps, hamstrings, and glutes. They also help improve balance and stability. 3 sets of 10 reps per leg are recommended.

- Calf Raises: Specific for strengthening the calf muscles. Perform 3 sets of 12-15 reps.

These exercises should be executed with attention to form, ensuring that the movements are controlled and muscles are engaged correctly. Similar to the upper body routine, variations of these exercises can be incorporated to provide a comprehensive lower body workout.

Advanced Options

For those looking to further intensify their workouts, advanced techniques can be employed:

- Supersets: This involves performing two exercises back-to-back with no rest in between. For example, doing a set of bench presses immediately followed by a set of pull-ups.

- Drop Sets: Start with a heavier weight and perform reps until failure, then immediately drop to a lighter weight and continue to failure. This can be applied to exercises like bicep curls or squats.

- Isolation Exercises: These exercises target specific muscles or muscle groups. Examples include tricep pushdowns for the upper body and leg curls for the lower body.

These advanced techniques are beneficial for pushing muscles beyond their usual capacity, leading to increased strength and muscle gains. They should be incorporated judiciously to avoid overtraining and ensure proper recovery.

Incorporating these workouts into an upper/lower split allows for focused and effective training sessions, with each muscle group receiving adequate attention and recovery time. Whether following the basic routines or incorporating advanced techniques, the upper/lower split offers a structured path to achieving strength and muscle development goals.

Ideal Candidates for the Upper/Lower Split

The upper/lower split workout regimen is an excellent choice for a specific segment of the fitness population. This split, dividing workouts into upper and lower body sessions, is particularly well-suited for those who have moved beyond the beginner stage and are looking for more specialized training. It is also ideal for individuals with specific strength goals, athletes focused on symmetry, and those who have a moderate amount of time to dedicate to exercise.

Intermediate to advanced fitness enthusiasts find the upper/lower split particularly beneficial. Once the basic principles of strength training are mastered and the initial phase of muscle adaptation has occurred, these individuals often seek a more targeted approach to training. The upper/lower split allows them to concentrate more intensely on each muscle group, facilitating a deeper level of muscular development and strength gains. This split provides the opportunity to increase the volume and intensity of workouts for each specific muscle group, a key factor in advancing fitness levels.

Individuals with specific strength goals, such as increasing muscle mass or achieving certain strength benchmarks, will find the upper/lower split to be particularly conducive to their objectives. This split allows for a balanced approach to muscle development, ensuring that all major muscle groups are being worked evenly. By dividing the body into upper and lower segments, it ensures that both halves are receiving equal attention, avoiding the common pitfall of disproportionate development. This balance is crucial not only for aesthetic purposes but also for functional strength and injury prevention.

Athletes focused on symmetry also benefit greatly from the upper/lower split. Many sports require a balanced physique for optimal performance, and asymmetrical development can lead to imbalances and potential injuries. The upper/lower split ensures that athletes can target all muscle groups equally, promoting a symmetrical development that is often crucial in competitive sports. This focus on balanced development helps athletes improve their overall performance and reduce the risk of sport-specific injuries.

The upper/lower split is also suitable for those who have a moderate amount of time to dedicate to exercise. With four dedicated workout days - two upper body and two lower body - this split is efficient for those who can commit to a structured weekly routine but may not have the time for more frequent gym visits. This schedule allows for substantial workouts for each half of the body while providing enough rest and recovery time between sessions. It's an effective way to maximize workout time without requiring daily gym commitments, making it practical for those with busy lifestyles.

The upper/lower split is a versatile and effective training method that caters to a wide range of fitness enthusiasts. Its structured approach allows for focused and intense workouts, promoting significant strength gains and muscular development. Whether the goal is to build muscle, improve athletic performance, or simply achieve a balanced and symmetrical physique, the upper/lower split offers a practical and efficient pathway to these fitness objectives.

Example upper/lower split workouts

The upper/lower split workout regimen is a balanced and efficient approach to strength training, dividing workouts into upper and lower body sessions. This structure is particularly effective for those looking to enhance their muscle development, strength, and overall fitness. The split allows for focused training sessions, ensuring that each major muscle group receives the attention and intensity it needs for optimal growth and development.

For the upper body workout, the focus is on exercises that target the chest, shoulders, back, and arms. This could include a mix of compound movements that work multiple muscle groups simultaneously, providing a more efficient workout, and isolation exercises that focus on specific muscles. A typical upper body workout in the upper/lower split might look like this:

- Bench Press: A staple exercise for chest development. It also engages the triceps and shoulders. Start with 3 sets of 6-8 repetitions, focusing on lifting heavy while maintaining good form.

- Bent-Over Rows: Essential for building a strong back. Perform 3 sets of 6-8 reps, ensuring you pull with your back muscles rather than just your arms.

- Shoulder Press: Either with dumbbells or a barbell, this exercise targets the shoulders and triceps. Do 3 sets of 6-8 reps.

- Pull-Ups or Lat Pull-Downs: Great for the lats and overall upper body strength. Aim for 3 sets to failure if doing pull-ups or 3 sets of 8-10 reps for lat pull-downs.

- Bicep Curls: A focused movement for bicep development. Perform 3 sets of 8-12 reps.

- Tricep Dips or Tricep Pushdowns: Finish the workout with tricep-focused exercises, aiming for 3 sets of 8-12 reps.

For the lower body workout, the emphasis is on the quadriceps, hamstrings, glutes, and calves. These workouts typically involve heavy and intense leg exercises, capitalizing on the lower body's capacity for strength. An example of a lower body workout could include:

- Squats: The king of lower body exercises. Perform 3 sets of 6-8 reps, focusing on depth and form.

- Deadlifts: A full-body exercise that heavily involves the lower back, glutes, and hamstrings. Do 3 sets of 6-8 reps.

- Leg Press: Useful for targeting the quadriceps and glutes, especially when squats are too taxing. Aim for 3 sets of 10-12 reps.

- Lunges: Walking lunges or stationary lunges work the entire leg. Do 3 sets of 10 reps per leg.

- Leg Curls: Focus on the hamstrings with 3 sets of 10-12 reps.

- Calf Raises: Finish the session by targeting the calves with 3 sets of 15-20 reps.

These workouts in the upper/lower split allow for a balanced approach to strength training, ensuring that all major muscle groups are worked evenly and effectively. The split also provides enough flexibility for individuals to adjust exercises, sets, and reps according to their fitness levels and goals. For those looking to increase intensity, advanced techniques like supersets, drop sets, or increasing the weight can be incorporated.

Incorporating the upper/lower split into a weekly routine offers an effective way to build strength and muscle in a structured manner. By focusing on upper body exercises in one session and lower body exercises in another, it ensures comprehensive muscle development and adequate recovery time. This split is adaptable, allowing individuals to tailor their workouts to their specific needs, whether they're aiming to increase muscle mass, improve strength, or enhance overall fitness.

Push/Pull/Legs Split

The push/pull/legs split is a highly regarded and efficient workout structure that has gained substantial popularity in the fitness community. This method categorizes exercises based on primary movement patterns, creating a well-rounded and balanced training regimen. This split is particularly favored for its ability to optimize training while ensuring comprehensive muscle engagement.

The framework of the push/pull/legs split is straightforward yet effective. It divides workouts into three distinct categories: push workouts, pull workouts, and legs workouts. Push workouts focus on exercises that involve pushing movements, primarily targeting the chest, shoulders, and triceps. Typical exercises include bench presses, overhead presses, and push-ups. These workouts are designed to maximize the development of the anterior (front) upper body muscles.

Pull workouts, on the other hand, revolve around pulling movements. These sessions primarily engage the back, biceps, and forearms. Exercises commonly found in pull workouts include pull-ups, rows, and deadlifts. The emphasis is on the posterior (back) upper body muscles, ensuring a balanced development in conjunction with the push workouts.

Legs workouts are dedicated exclusively to the lower body. This category includes exercises that target the quadriceps, hamstrings, glutes, and calves. Key exercises in leg workouts include squats, lunges, and calf raises. These sessions are crucial for building lower body strength and symmetry with the upper body muscle groups.

Typically, the push/pull/legs split is executed over a three-day or six-day cycle. The three-day cycle is suitable for those with limited time or those who prefer longer recovery periods. It involves one day each for push, pull, and legs workouts, with rest or active recovery days in between. The six-day cycle doubles the frequency, allowing each muscle group to be worked twice a week. This higher frequency can lead to faster strength gains and muscle growth, but it requires a higher level of fitness and recovery capability.

One of the primary benefits of the push/pull/legs split is balanced muscle development. By categorizing workouts based on movement patterns, it ensures that all major muscle groups are worked evenly. This balanced approach prevents muscle imbalances and fosters a harmonious physique. It's particularly beneficial for those aiming for aesthetic improvements as well as functional strength.

Versatility is another significant advantage of this split. It can be adapted to various frequencies to accommodate different schedules and recovery needs. Whether an individual can commit to three days or six days of training per week, the push/pull/legs split can be modified accordingly. This flexibility makes it a viable option for a wide range of individuals, from busy professionals to dedicated athletes.

Focused intensity is a key characteristic of each workout day in the push/pull/legs split. By concentrating on specific muscle groups each session, it allows for a more intense and effective workout. This focus enhances muscle fatigue and growth within each group, leading to more efficient training sessions. It also allows for a higher volume of work for each muscle group, a critical factor for hypertrophy and strength gains.

Lastly, the split minimizes the chances of muscle overuse and fatigue. Since each muscle group is worked independently on different days, there's a reduced risk of overtraining. This separation allows for adequate recovery for each muscle group, which is crucial for muscle repair, growth, and overall workout effectiveness.

The push/pull/legs split is a structured approach to strength training, dividing workouts into three distinct categories – push, pull, and legs – each targeting specific muscle groups. This division allows for an intense focus on each muscle group, leading to more effective training sessions and balanced muscle development.

Push Workout

The push workout targets muscles involved in pushing movements, primarily the chest, shoulders, and triceps. This workout typically includes:

- Bench Press: A cornerstone exercise for chest development. It also engages the triceps and shoulders. Start with 3-4 sets of 6-10 repetitions, using a weight that challenges the muscles while maintaining proper form.

- Overhead Press: This exercise targets the shoulders (deltoids) and also works the triceps. Perform 3-4 sets of 6-10 reps, choosing a weight that allows for full range of motion.

- Tricep Dips: These focus on the triceps, and can be performed using parallel bars or a bench. Aim for 3 sets of 8-12 reps.

- Incline Bench Press: This variation targets the upper chest and shoulders more than the flat bench press. Perform 3 sets of 6-10 reps.

- Side Lateral Raises: Excellent for isolating the side deltoids. Do 3 sets of 10-15 reps using lighter weights for proper form.

The push workout effectively exhausts the upper body pushing muscles, leading to improved strength and size in these areas.

Pull Workout

The pull workout focuses on the upper body pulling muscles: the back, biceps, and forearms. Key exercises include:

- Deadlifts: A compound movement that targets the entire back, including the latissimus dorsi, rhomboids, and traps. Perform 3-4 sets of 6-8 reps with a challenging weight.

- Pull-Ups: Excellent for back and bicep development. Aim for 3 sets of as many reps as possible. If too difficult, assisted pull-ups or lat pull-downs can be substituted.

- Barbell Rows: Focus on the middle and lower back. Perform 3-4 sets of 6-10 reps, ensuring you're pulling with your back muscles.

- Bicep Curls: Can be done with dumbbells or a barbell. Aim for 3 sets of 8-12 reps.

- Face Pulls: Target the rear deltoids and upper back. Perform 3 sets of 12-15 reps.

The pull workout thoroughly works the back and bicep muscles, promoting balanced development with the pushing muscles.

Legs Workout

The legs workout is dedicated to the lower body, targeting the quadriceps, hamstrings, glutes, and calves. A typical legs workout includes:

- Squats: The most comprehensive lower body exercise. Perform 3-4 sets of 6-10 reps, focusing on depth and maintaining form.

- Lunges: Work the quads, hamstrings, and glutes. Do 3 sets of 10 reps per leg.

- Leg Press: An alternative or addition to squats, targeting the quads and glutes. Aim for 3 sets of 10-12 reps.

- Romanian Deadlifts: Focus on the hamstrings and glutes. Perform 3 sets of 8-10 reps.

- Calf Raises: Essential for developing the calf muscles. Do 3 sets of 12-15 reps.

The legs workout ensures that the lower body is not neglected, providing a balanced approach to full-body development.

Each of these workouts in the push/pull/legs split allows for targeted muscle development and strength gains. By focusing on specific muscle groups in each session, the split ensures comprehensive development across all major muscle groups. The routine can be adapted in terms of the number of sets, repetitions, and weights used to suit individual fitness levels and goals.

Ideal Candidates for the Push/Pull/Legs Split

The push/pull/legs split is a highly versatile workout regimen well-suited for certain types of trainees due to its specific structure and intense focus on different muscle groups. This split is ideal for intermediate and advanced trainees, individuals with flexible schedules, and those with goal-specific training targets such as building strength, hypertrophy, or muscle definition.

Intermediate and Advanced Trainees

Intermediate and advanced trainees often reach a point in their fitness journey where generalized workouts no longer yield the same level of results as before. These individuals require a more specific and intense focus on each muscle group to continue progressing. The push/pull/legs split meets this need perfectly, as it allows for an intense workout of each muscle group before moving on to the next. This split provides the opportunity to focus on heavier lifts and more complex movements that are crucial for continued muscle development and strength gains. Since each workout day is dedicated to a specific set of muscles, it's easier to target weaknesses and work on specific areas for balanced, overall development.

Individuals with a Flexible Schedule

The push/pull/legs split is highly adaptable, making it suitable for individuals with varying schedules. For those who can commit to a six-day workout cycle, this split allows each muscle group to be worked twice a week, accelerating progress in strength and hypertrophy. Alternatively, for those with tighter schedules or who require more recovery time, the split can be adjusted to a three-day cycle. This flexibility is a significant advantage, as it allows individuals to tailor their workout routine to their lifestyle without compromising the effectiveness of their training program. The ability to adjust the frequency also means that the split can accommodate changes in an individual's life, be it due to work, family commitments, or other responsibilities.

Goal-Specific Trainees

Individuals with specific fitness goals such as building strength, increasing muscle size (hypertrophy), or enhancing overall muscle definition find the push/pull/legs split particularly beneficial. This workout structure allows for focused and intense training sessions that are key to these goals. For strength and hypertrophy, the split supports high-volume and high-intensity workouts, crucial for stimulating muscle growth and strength improvement. The separation of muscle groups ensures that each group is thoroughly exhausted in its workout, an essential factor in muscle hypertrophy.

Furthermore, for those focusing on muscle definition, this split allows for targeted exercises that can sculpt and define various muscle groups. The ability to concentrate on specific areas in each workout ensures that all muscles are developed evenly, contributing to a more defined and aesthetic physique.

The Bro Split

The "bro split" stands as a classic, time-tested approach to strength training and bodybuilding. Its roots run deep in the fitness community, where it has been embraced for its intense focus on individual muscle groups. The bro split dedicates each day of the week to training a specific muscle group, typically spread over five to six days. This structure allows for highly focused and intense workouts for each muscle group, providing ample time for recovery before the same group is worked again.

The bro split's primary appeal lies in its intense muscle focus. This split allows for a high volume and intensity of training for each muscle group. For example, a typical bro split routine might dedicate one day entirely to chest exercises, another to back, and so on. This approach ensures that each muscle group is thoroughly worked during its dedicated session, leading to significant muscle fatigue and subsequent growth. This focus is particularly beneficial for those looking to increase muscle size and definition, as it allows for targeted development of each muscle group.

Simplicity is another key advantage of the bro split. Its straightforward structure is easy to understand and follow, making it an attractive option for both beginners and experienced gym-goers. This simplicity also aids in maintaining a routine, as there's no confusion about what muscle group to work on any given day. For beginners, it provides a clear roadmap for navigating the gym, and for the experienced, it allows for a well-structured approach to their training.

Customization is a significant aspect of the bro split. It allows for a high degree of personalization in choosing exercises for each muscle group. Depending on individual preferences, goals, and needs, exercises can be selected to target different aspects of each muscle group. For instance, on chest day, one could focus on flat bench presses, incline presses, and flyes, tailoring the workout to specific chest areas.

One of the most critical aspects of the bro split is the recovery time it affords each muscle group. By working each muscle group intensely once a week, the split provides a full week of recovery before that group is worked again. This extended recovery period is beneficial for muscle growth and repair, as muscles need time to recover and grow after being subjected to intense training. It's during this recovery period that the actual process of muscle building occurs.

The bro split's focus on one muscle group per day also allows for a more extended workout for each group. This can lead to increased muscle exhaustion and, consequently, growth. For example, dedicating an entire session to the back allows for a variety of exercises targeting different back parts, such as the latissimus dorsi, rhomboids, and trapezius muscles. This variety ensures comprehensive development of the muscle group and can lead to more pronounced muscle gains.

Additionally, the bro split's structure aids in preventing burnout and overtraining. By concentrating on one muscle group per session, the risk of overworking a muscle group is significantly reduced. This approach allows for more focused energy and effort during each workout, as only one major muscle group is being taxed per session.

However, the bro split requires a significant time commitment, as it typically involves training five to six days a week. This commitment can be challenging for those with busy schedules or limited time for gym sessions. Despite this, for those who can dedicate the necessary time, the bro split offers a highly effective way to build muscle and strength.

Example Workout Routine

The bro split routine is a classic approach in bodybuilding and strength training circles, targeting one major muscle group each day of the week. This approach allows for an intense focus on each muscle group, providing ample time for recovery before the same group is worked again. A sample weekly bro split routine can be structured as follows:

Monday: Chest Day

- Bench Press: Begin with 3-4 sets of 6-8 reps. The bench press is a staple in chest development, targeting the pectorals, triceps, and front deltoids.

- Incline Dumbbell Press: Perform 3 sets of 8-10 reps. This exercise focuses on the upper chest, promoting a balanced chest development.

- Chest Flyes: Do 3 sets of 10-12 reps. Flyes help to stretch and isolate the chest muscles, enhancing muscle definition.

Tuesday: Back Day

- Pull-Ups: Aim for 3-4 sets to failure. Pull-ups are excellent for overall back development, particularly targeting the latissimus dorsi.

- Bent-Over Rows: Complete 3 sets of 6-8 reps. This exercise strengthens the middle back muscles and contributes to overall back thickness.

- Lat Pulldowns: Do 3 sets of 8-10 reps. Lat pulldowns focus on the width of the back, particularly the lats.

Wednesday: Shoulders Day

- Overhead Press: Start with 3-4 sets of 6-8 reps. The overhead press is crucial for building overall shoulder strength and size.

- Lateral Raises: Perform 3 sets of 10-12 reps. Lateral raises target the side deltoids, essential for shoulder width and definition.

- Front Raises: Do 3 sets of 10-12 reps. This exercise targets the front deltoids, rounding out shoulder development.

Thursday: Arms Day

- Bicep Curls: Perform 3 sets of 8-10 reps. Bicep curls are fundamental for building arm size and strength.

- Tricep Extensions: Complete 3 sets of 8-10 reps. Tricep extensions target the triceps muscles, crucial for overall arm development.

- Hammer Curls: Do 3 sets of 10-12 reps. Hammer curls focus on the brachialis and brachioradialis, enhancing arm thickness and strength.

Friday: Legs Day

- Squats: Begin with 3-4 sets of 6-8 reps. Squats are essential for overall leg development, particularly the quadriceps and glutes.

- Deadlifts: Perform 3 sets of 6-8 reps. Deadlifts target the entire posterior chain, including the hamstrings, glutes, and lower back.

- Leg Presses: Complete 3 sets of 10-12 reps. The leg press is a great complement to squats, targeting the quads and glutes with less strain on the lower back.

Saturday: Rest or Optional Focus on a Weak Muscle Group

This day can be used for rest or to focus on a weaker muscle group that needs additional attention. If choosing to train, select 2-3 exercises for the targeted muscle group and perform a moderate workout, being mindful not to overtrain.

Sunday: Rest

Dedicate this day to complete rest, allowing your body to recover, repair, and grow stronger. Rest is a critical component of any training routine, particularly one as intense as the bro split.

This sample weekly bro split routine offers a comprehensive approach to muscle building, with each day dedicated to enhancing a specific muscle group. It's crucial to ensure proper form and adequate recovery between sets and exercises. Additionally, listen to your body and make adjustments as needed based on your recovery and overall fitness progress.

Ideal Candidates for the Bro Split

The bro split, known for its intense focus on individual muscle groups, is a workout regimen that resonates with specific segments of the fitness community. Its structure, which dedicates each day to a different muscle group, makes it particularly suitable for certain types of individuals, such as bodybuilders, experienced lifters, those with flexible schedules, and recovery-oriented trainees.

Bodybuilders and Muscle Builders

The bro split is ideal for bodybuilders and those focusing on muscle hypertrophy and definition. This split's structure allows for an intensive workout on each muscle group, leading to significant muscle fatigue and growth. By dedicating an entire day to one muscle group, individuals can perform a high volume of exercises targeting various aspects of that muscle, which is crucial for hypertrophy. The bro split also allows for a focus on muscle definition. The ability to concentrate on one muscle group at a time enables lifters to perform isolation exercises that enhance muscle shape and definition, a key goal in bodybuilding.

Experienced Lifters

Experienced lifters, who already have a solid foundation in strength training, find the bro split particularly effective. These individuals are typically capable of handling high-volume and high-intensity workouts that the bro split demands. Having developed a base level of strength and muscle endurance, they can benefit from the intensive nature of the bro split, which can lead to further strength gains and muscle development. Experienced lifters often have the technique and stamina necessary to withstand the rigors of this type of training, making the bro split a suitable choice for their advanced training needs.

Those with Flexible Schedules

The bro split is best suited for individuals who can dedicate five to six days a week to their workout routine. Due to its structure, the bro split requires a significant time commitment, with each workout day focusing on a different muscle group. This frequency is essential for the split's effectiveness, as it ensures that each muscle group is thoroughly worked each week. Individuals with the flexibility to commit to this type of schedule will find the bro split to be a practical and efficient way to structure their workouts.

Recovery-Oriented Trainees

Trainees who require or prefer longer recovery periods for each muscle group will find the bro split beneficial. Since each muscle group is worked intensely only once a week, there is ample time for recovery before that group is targeted again. This extended recovery time can be advantageous for muscle repair and growth. For individuals who need more time to recover due to their physiological makeup, age, or other factors, the bro split provides the necessary rest period for each muscle

The 5x5 Split

The 5x5 training program is a paradigm of strength training, valued for its straightforward yet highly effective approach. Centering on five sets of five repetitions of key compound lifts, this program is not just about building muscle; it's a comprehensive method to enhance overall strength and athletic performance. The 5x5 program is a testament to the principle that in simplicity lies power. This regimen revolves around a select few compound exercises, each performed with heavy weights. The core idea is to engage multiple muscle groups simultaneously, making every session both time-efficient and potent.

Compound exercises are the linchpin of the 5x5 program. These movements, such as squats, deadlifts, bench presses, and overhead presses, work several muscle groups at once. Unlike isolation exercises that target individual muscles, compound movements recruit large muscle areas, offering a more holistic approach to strength building. This method not only accelerates muscle growth but also enhances functional strength – the kind of strength that is useful in everyday life.

Squats, for instance, engage the quadriceps, hamstrings, glutes, lower back, and core, making them an incredibly effective lower body exercise. The deadlift, another staple of the 5x5 program, works almost every major muscle group, including the back, glutes, legs, and core. The bench press and overhead press are critical for developing the upper body, targeting the chest, shoulders, and triceps. These exercises combined provide a balanced workout that strengthens the entire body.

A key feature of the 5x5 program is its emphasis on progressive overload, a crucial principle in strength training. Progressive overload involves gradually increasing the weight lifted to challenge the muscles continuously. This approach is critical for muscle growth and strength improvement. In the context of the 5x5 program, once an individual can complete five sets of five reps with a certain weight, they increase the weight slightly in the next workout. This gradual increase ensures steady progress and minimizes the risk of injury.

The 5x5 program is also marked by its simplicity, both in terms of the exercises involved and its implementation. With only a handful of exercises to focus on, it's easier for individuals to track their progress and maintain consistency. This simplicity is especially beneficial for beginners who can often be overwhelmed by more complex routines. For the experienced lifter, the straightforward nature of the program provides a clear structure for continued development.

However, the simplicity of the 5x5 program doesn't imply that it's easy. The workouts can be quite challenging, particularly as the weights increase. The five sets of five reps scheme requires a significant amount of physical and mental endurance. This aspect of the program builds not just muscle, but also grit and determination, qualities that are invaluable in any fitness journey.

The 5x5 program is also adaptable. While the traditional 5x5 split focuses on three workouts per week, it can be adjusted according to individual needs and schedules. For example, someone with more time and recovery capability might add a fourth day focusing on accessory exercises or additional cardiovascular work. Conversely, for someone pressed for time, the program can be condensed into two longer workouts per week.

This training regimen is particularly well-suited for those looking to gain strength in a structured and measurable way. It is ideal for beginners to intermediate lifters, though advanced lifters can also benefit significantly by returning to this fundamental strength-building approach. The 5x5 program is not just about lifting weights; it's about building a solid foundation upon which other fitness goals can be achieved.

In essence, the 5x5 program is a powerful tool in the arsenal of strength training. Its focus on compound movements, progressive overload, and simplicity makes it an effective and efficient method for building strength and muscle. This program proves that sometimes, the most straightforward approaches can be the most impactful, providing a clear path to greater strength and overall fitness.

Example 5x5 Workouts

The 5x5 workout program, renowned for its simplicity and effectiveness, revolves around two primary workout routines – Workout A and Workout B. These routines are alternated three times a week, focusing on major compound movements that engage multiple muscle groups. The essence of the 5x5 program lies in its structured approach, performing five sets of five reps for each exercise, except for deadlifts, which due to their intensity, are typically performed for one set of five reps.

Workout A

- Squat: The squat is a fundamental exercise in the 5x5 program. It targets the quadriceps, hamstrings, glutes, lower back, and core. For the 5x5 routine, you perform five sets of five reps. The focus should be on maintaining proper form, keeping the back straight, and driving through the heels. As a full-body compound movement, it not only builds lower body strength but also contributes to overall muscle growth and development.

- Bench Press: Next in Workout A is the bench press, which primarily works the chest muscles (pectorals), as well as the triceps and shoulders (deltoids). Again, five sets of five reps are performed. Proper form includes lying flat on the bench, feet firmly on the ground, and controlling the barbell as it's lowered to the chest and pushed back up. The bench press is key for upper body strength and is a staple in strength training.

- Barbell Row: The barbell row focuses on the upper back, including the latissimus dorsi, rhomboids, and trapezius muscles, as well as the biceps. It's crucial for maintaining balance in the body's musculature, countering the pushing movements of the bench press. Perform five sets of five reps, maintaining a bent-over position with a straight back, pulling the barbell towards the lower ribs, and then lowering it under control.

Workout B

- Squat: As in Workout A, the squat is also the first exercise in Workout B, highlighting its importance in the program. The same approach is followed – five sets of five reps, focusing on depth, form, and control. Consistent performance of squats is crucial for lower body strength and overall athletic ability.

- Overhead Press: The overhead press, or military press, targets the shoulders, triceps, and upper back. This exercise is performed standing, pressing the barbell from shoulder height above the head. Five sets of five reps are done, ensuring that each rep involves a full range of motion from shoulders to lockout above the head. The overhead press is essential for building strong, functional shoulders and arms.

- Deadlift: The deadlift is a powerful compound exercise that targets the entire posterior chain, including the hamstrings, glutes, lower and upper back. Due to its intensity, only one set of five reps is performed in the 5x5 program. Proper form is crucial to avoid injury – keeping the back straight, lifting with the legs and hips, and keeping the barbell close to the body throughout the lift.

In both Workout A and Workout B, the weights used should be challenging yet manageable to complete all sets and reps with proper form. The 5x5 program is designed for progressive overload, meaning that as you grow stronger, you should gradually increase the weight used in each exercise. This progression is key to the effectiveness of the 5x5 program, driving consistent strength and muscle gains.

These workouts encapsulate the essence of strength training – focusing on major compound movements, challenging the body, and promoting growth. The simplicity of the 5x5 program makes it highly effective, ensuring a balanced approach to building foundational strength.

Benefits of Strength-Focused Splits

Strength-focused workout splits, particularly the renowned 5x5 program, offer a plethora of benefits for a wide demographic, ranging from beginners to seasoned athletes. These splits, known for their simplicity and effectiveness, are designed to build foundational strength that is applicable to both sports and daily activities. They provide a structured pathway for increasing muscle strength, enhancing bone and joint health, boosting metabolism, and improving athletic performance.

One of the most significant benefits of strength-focused splits like the 5x5 program is the increased muscle strength. This type of training regimen emphasizes heavy lifting with compound movements, which are key to developing overall muscular strength. Compound exercises such as squats, deadlifts, and bench presses target multiple muscle groups simultaneously, allowing for a more efficient strength-building workout. Increased muscle strength is not only beneficial for enhancing physical appearance but is also crucial in improving daily functional abilities, such as lifting heavy objects, pushing or pulling items, and maintaining overall body stability.

Another crucial benefit of these workout splits is their positive impact on bone and joint health. Strength training is known to enhance bone density, which is especially important as one ages. Regularly performing weight-bearing exercises helps in combating age-related bone loss, reducing the risk of osteoporosis, and other bone-related conditions. Furthermore, by strengthening the muscles around the joints, these workouts contribute to joint stability, which can help prevent injuries and improve overall joint health.

Metabolic boost is another key advantage of engaging in strength-focused workout splits. Strength training has been shown to elevate metabolism, aiding in fat loss and muscle maintenance. This metabolic increase occurs because muscle tissue burns more calories at rest compared to fat tissue. Therefore, by increasing muscle mass through strength training, one can elevate their resting metabolic rate, making it easier to maintain a healthy body weight or lose fat if that's a personal goal.

Improved athletic performance is a direct outcome of engaging in a strength-focused training regimen.

Strength gains achieved through these workouts translate to better performance in almost every athletic endeavor, be it running, swimming, cycling, or team sports. Enhanced muscle strength and endurance allow athletes to perform at a higher level, improve their technique, and reduce the risk of sport-related injuries.

The 5x5 workout split, in particular, is excellent for strength training beginners due to its straightforward approach. This program simplifies strength training into a manageable format, focusing on a few key exercises and requiring only three workouts per week. For someone new to strength training, this simplicity eliminates the often overwhelming complexity of more intricate workout routines, providing a clear and concise pathway to gaining strength and confidence in the gym.

Athletes, regardless of their sport, can benefit immensely from the 5x5 split. For competitive sports, a strong foundation of muscular strength is often a prerequisite for peak performance. The 5x5 program offers a focused approach to building this foundation, ensuring athletes develop the strength needed to excel in their respective sports.

Individuals with limited time find the 5x5 split ideal. Since the program is designed for efficiency, requiring only three days a week, it's suitable for those with busy schedules. Each workout in the 5x5 program is concise yet effective, focusing on a few compound exercises that provide a full-body workout in a relatively short period.

Lastly, the 5x5 split is suitable for anyone seeking to improve their overall functional fitness and core strength. This program not only builds muscle in the traditional sense but also enhances the body's ability to perform everyday activities more efficiently and with less risk of injury. The focus on compound movements ensures that the core and stabilizing muscles are engaged, which is crucial for overall functional strength.

In summary, strength-focused splits, and particularly the 5x5 program, are beneficial for a wide range of individuals. They offer a structured approach to increasing muscle strength, enhancing bone and joint health, boosting metabolism, and improving athletic performance. These splits are ideal for beginners, athletes, individuals with limited time, and those seeking functional strength, making them a versatile tool in achieving various fitness goals.

Hybrid and Custom Splits

Hybrid and custom workout splits represent an innovative approach to fitness training, offering unparalleled flexibility and personalization. These types of splits are tailored to individual needs, blending elements from traditional workout splits to create a unique fitness regimen. This approach is particularly beneficial for individuals with specific goals, varied interests, or unique scheduling needs.

The concept of hybrid and custom splits is rooted in the idea that no one-size-fits-all solution exists for fitness training. Every individual has unique goals, preferences, body types, and lifestyles, all of which should be considered when designing a workout plan. Hybrid splits allow for the combination of different training styles and methodologies. For example, someone might combine elements of a body part split (like the bro split) with full-body workout days. This could mean dedicating specific days to focus intensely on one muscle group while incorporating full-body workouts on other days for balanced development.

Designing a custom split requires a thoughtful assessment of personal goals. For instance, someone aiming to build strength might focus more on heavy compound exercises, whereas someone interested in muscle toning might incorporate a mix of weightlifting and high-repetition training. Endurance enhancement might call for integrating cardiovascular exercises, while weight loss could involve a combination of strength training and high-intensity interval training (HIIT). Understanding these goals is crucial in shaping the structure of the workout split.

An individual's lifestyle and time availability play a significant role in designing a custom split. For those with demanding jobs or family commitments, a workout split needs to be efficient and flexible. For example, a busy professional might opt for shorter, more intense workout sessions or fewer training days with longer workouts. Similarly, someone with a more flexible schedule might choose a split that allows for more frequent but shorter sessions.

Recovery capability is another critical factor. The workout split should provide enough time for rest and muscle recovery, which is essential for growth and preventing overtraining. This consideration might lead to alternating between intense workout days and lighter or active recovery days.

The incorporation of varied training styles is a hallmark of hybrid and custom splits. This variety not only keeps the workouts interesting and challenging but also ensures that all major muscle groups are worked. For instance, someone might combine powerlifting exercises for strength with bodybuilding techniques for hypertrophy and some elements of functional training for overall fitness.

Ensuring comprehensive development of all muscle groups is essential in a hybrid or custom split. This means that while the split might focus on certain areas or goals, it should still provide a balanced workout regimen. For example, if someone's primary focus is on upper body strength, they should still incorporate lower body and core exercises to prevent imbalances and maintain overall fitness.

Hybrid and custom splits also allow for specific tailoring to address individual weaknesses or preferences. For example, if someone has a weaker lower back, they can incorporate specific exercises to strengthen that area. Similarly, if someone prefers certain types of exercises or equipment, those can be integrated into their custom plan.

Flexibility in adjusting the split over time is another advantage. As individuals progress in their fitness journey, their goals and needs might change. A custom or hybrid split can be easily modified to accommodate these changes, whether it's increasing the intensity, changing the focus, or incorporating new exercises.

In summary, hybrid and custom workout splits offer a personalized approach to fitness training. By blending elements from different splits and tailoring them to individual needs and goals, these splits provide a flexible and effective way to achieve fitness objectives. Whether it's building strength, enhancing muscle tone, improving endurance, or losing weight, hybrid and custom splits offer a tailored pathway to reach these goals while ensuring a balanced and comprehensive approach to physical development.

Examples of Hybrid Splits

Hybrid workout splits represent a modern and adaptable approach to fitness, combining elements from various established training methods to suit individual needs and goals. These hybrid splits provide the flexibility to focus on specific areas while maintaining a holistic approach to fitness. Let's delve into some examples of hybrid splits and how they can be structured.

Upper/Lower + Full Body Split

This hybrid split merges the focus of an upper/lower split with the comprehensive approach of full-body workouts. In a typical week, a trainee might alternate between upper/lower body days and full-body workout days. This structure allows for concentrated effort on specific muscle groups during the upper/lower days, while full-body days ensure all muscle groups are engaged within the same session.

For example, the week might begin with an upper body workout on Monday, focusing on exercises like bench presses and pull-ups. Tuesday could then shift to a lower body workout with squats and deadlifts. Wednesday might be a rest or active recovery day, followed by a full-body workout on Thursday, incorporating a mix of upper and lower body exercises. The cycle could then repeat or mix in additional rest days, depending on the individual's recovery needs and schedule.

Push/Pull/Legs + Bro Split Hybrid

This hybrid split combines the push/pull/legs framework with elements of the bro split, dedicating specific days to individual muscle groups. This structure allows for a balance between focused muscle group training and comprehensive workouts. For example, a week might start with a push workout (chest, shoulders, triceps) on Monday, followed by a pull workout (back, biceps) on Tuesday, and a legs workout (quadriceps, hamstrings, calves) on Wednesday.

The latter part of the week could then shift to a bro split approach, with Thursday dedicated to chest, Friday to back, and Saturday to arms. This hybrid split allows for intense focus on each muscle group while still maintaining the balanced approach of the push/pull/legs split.

5x5 + Functional Training Split

This hybrid combines the strength-focused 5x5 program, known for its simplicity and effectiveness in building strength, with functional training exercises to enhance athletic performance. The 5x5 portion of the workout, which includes exercises like squats, deadlifts, and bench presses, could be performed three days a week – for example, Monday, Wednesday, and Friday.

On alternate days, functional training exercises could be incorporated. These exercises focus on movements that mimic daily activities or sports-specific movements, improving overall athletic ability and functional strength. Such workouts might include kettlebell swings, medicine ball throws, or plyometric exercises. This combination ensures the development of raw strength while also enhancing agility, balance, and coordination.

Endurance and Strength Split

This hybrid split is ideal for those looking to balance endurance training with strength training. It's particularly suitable for athletes in sports that require both strength and endurance, such as obstacle course racing or triathlon. In this split, endurance training sessions (such as running, cycling, or swimming) could be alternated with strength training workouts.

A typical week might include endurance training on Monday, Wednesday, and Friday, focusing on different aspects such as speed, distance, and recovery pace. Strength training sessions on Tuesday, Thursday, and Saturday would then focus on full-body strength workouts, ensuring that all major muscle groups are targeted. This split allows for the development of both cardiovascular endurance and muscular strength, contributing to overall athletic performance and fitness.

In summary, hybrid workout splits offer a versatile approach to fitness training, allowing individuals to tailor their workouts to their specific goals and preferences. Whether the goal is to build muscle, enhance athletic performance, or achieve a balance of strength and endurance, hybrid splits provide a structured yet flexible framework to achieve these objectives. These examples demonstrate the adaptability of hybrid splits, accommodating a wide range of fitness levels and goals.

The Benefits of Personalized Splits

Personalized workout splits, encompassing both hybrid and custom splits, represent a cutting-edge approach in the fitness realm. These splits are designed to cater directly to individual needs, preferences, and goals, offering a multitude of benefits that standard, one-size-fits-all routines fail to provide. The primary advantages of these personalized splits include targeted results, adaptability, enhanced motivation, and the potential for holistic development.

Targeted Results

One of the most compelling reasons for adopting a personalized workout split is the ability to achieve targeted results. Each individual has unique fitness goals, whether it's building muscle, increasing endurance, losing weight, or improving athletic performance. A personalized split allows for the creation of a workout routine that directly aligns with these specific objectives. For instance, someone aiming for muscle hypertrophy might focus more on weightlifting and high-volume workouts, while an endurance athlete would integrate more cardiovascular exercises into their split. This tailored approach ensures that every minute spent in the gym is optimized towards achieving the desired outcome.

Adaptability

Personalized workout splits offer unparalleled adaptability. Life is dynamic, and circumstances can change rapidly, impacting one's ability to stick to a rigid workout schedule. Custom splits can be easily modified to accommodate changes in lifestyle, time availability, or fitness level. For example, if an individual's work schedule becomes more demanding, the split can be adjusted to shorter, more intense workouts, or if an injury occurs, the routine can be altered to focus on recovery and exercises that do not strain the affected area. This flexibility is not just a matter of convenience; it's crucial for maintaining consistent progress in the face of life's unpredictable nature.

Enhanced Motivation

Customization in workout routines keeps the training process engaging and relevant, which is vital for sustained motivation. Doing the same exercises week after week can lead to boredom and a plateau in progress. Personalized splits allow for variety and creativity in workouts, keeping the individual engaged and challenged. This might involve mixing different types of training, such as incorporating elements of powerlifting into a bodybuilding routine or blending yoga and mobility work into a strength training program. This variety not only makes workouts more enjoyable but also ensures that different aspects of fitness are being developed.

Holistic Development

Personalized splits offer the potential for a well-rounded approach to fitness. Standard workout routines often focus on specific goals, like muscle building or cardiovascular endurance, which can lead to imbalances in development. Custom splits, on the other hand, can be designed to address all aspects of fitness – strength, endurance, flexibility, and balance – leading to a more holistic development. This approach is crucial for overall health and wellness and can significantly reduce the risk of injuries that often result from imbalances or overemphasis on certain types of training.

Ideal Candidates for Hybrid and Custom Splits

- Experienced Gym-Goers: Individuals who have spent considerable time in the gym and understand their bodies and fitness needs are ideal candidates for hybrid and custom splits. These individuals have the knowledge to mix different training styles effectively, tailoring their routines to their evolving goals and preferences.

- Goal-Specific Athletes: Athletes training for specific sports or events require workout routines that address the particular demands of their sport. Personalized splits allow these athletes to focus on the aspects of fitness that will most enhance their performance in their chosen sport, be it strength, speed, agility, or endurance.

- People with Unique Schedules: Those whose lifestyles demand flexibility in their workout routines can greatly benefit from custom splits. Be it working parents, traveling professionals, or students balancing studies and fitness, personalized splits offer the adaptability needed to fit workouts into diverse and often changing schedules.

- Fitness Enthusiasts Seeking Variety: For those who enjoy exploring different aspects of fitness and dislike the monotony of standard routines, personalized splits offer an opportunity to diversify their training. This might involve experimenting with new exercises, incorporating different training methodologies, or adjusting the routine to align with changing fitness interests.

Personalized workout splits offer a range of benefits that standard workout programs often fail to provide. Their ability to deliver targeted results, adaptability to changing circumstances, enhancement of motivation through customization, and the potential for holistic development make them an excellent choice for a wide array of individuals. From experienced gym-goers and specific-goal athletes to people with unique schedules and fitness enthusiasts seeking variety, personalized workout splits present a flexible and effective solution for achieving diverse fitness goals.

Navigating the Complexities of Workout Splits

In the realm of fitness and bodybuilding, workout splits are a fundamental concept, often surrounded by questions and misconceptions. This chapter aims to provide clarity and guidance on navigating the complexities of workout splits, offering answers to frequently asked questions, debunking common misconceptions, and providing tips to avoid typical mistakes.

Frequently Asked Questions

- Changing Workout Splits: How often one should change their workout split depends on several factors, including progress, boredom, and adaptation. Generally, it's advisable to change your split every 8-12 weeks to prevent plateaus and keep the training stimulus fresh. However, if a split is still yielding results and remains enjoyable, it's perfectly fine to stick with it longer.

- Cardio on Rest Days: Incorporating light to moderate cardio on rest days can be beneficial. It keeps the body active and can aid in recovery by increasing blood flow to the muscles. However, it's important to ensure that this doesn't compromise recovery by being too intense or lengthy.

- Necessity of Specific Splits for Results: While workout splits can be highly effective, they are not the only way to achieve fitness results. The key to success in any training program is consistency, proper nutrition, and a workout plan that aligns with one's goals, whether it's a split routine or a full-body approach.

- Determining the Right Split: Choosing the right workout split involves considering factors such as fitness goals, experience level, schedule, and personal preferences. It's essential to select a split that not only aligns with your goals but is also realistic in terms of your time commitment and enjoyment.

- Combining Different Workout Splits: Yes, it's possible to combine different types of workout splits. This approach, often seen in hybrid splits, allows for more customization and can address specific training goals or preferences. For example, one could combine elements of a push/pull/legs split with full-body workouts.

Debunking Common Misconceptions

- More Gym Time Equals Better Results: Quality over quantity is crucial in fitness. Longer or more frequent gym sessions don't necessarily lead to better results and can sometimes lead to overtraining or burnout.

- Sticking to One Workout Split: While consistency is important, it's not mandatory to stick to one workout split indefinitely. Changing your split can provide new challenges and stimuli to the muscles, aiding in continued progress.

- Heavier Weights Are Always Better: While lifting heavy is important for strength and muscle building, it's not the only way to achieve results. Different rep ranges and intensities have their place in a well-rounded fitness program.

- Rest Days for Complete Inactivity: Rest days are essential for recovery, but they don't necessarily mean complete inactivity. Active recovery, such as light cardio, stretching, or yoga, can be beneficial.

Tips to Avoid Common Mistakes in Workout Splits

- Not Allowing Adequate Recovery: Underestimating the importance of rest can lead to overtraining and hinder progress. It's essential to include rest days in your split and listen to your body for signs of fatigue.

- Ignoring Nutrition and Hydration: Both play a crucial role in supporting your workout split. Proper nutrition fuels your workouts and aids in recovery, while staying hydrated is key for overall health and exercise performance.

- Lack of Consistency: Sticking to a workout routine is fundamental for seeing results. Consistency trumps perfection, and being regular with your workouts is more important than waiting for the 'perfect' time or conditions.

- Imbalanced Training: Focusing too much on certain muscle groups and neglecting others can lead to imbalances and injuries. Ensure your split addresses all major muscle groups evenly.

- Ignoring Form and Technique: Proper form and technique are essential for preventing injuries and getting the most out of your exercises. Always prioritize form over the amount of weight lifted.

Fine-Tuning Your Workout Split

- Listening to Your Body: Be attentive to what your body tells you. If you feel overly fatigued or experience pain (beyond normal muscle soreness), it may be time to adjust your split or intensity.

- Seeking Professional Guidance: Especially when starting a new split or if you hit a plateau, consulting with a fitness professional can provide valuable insights and guidance.

Incorporating Feedback into Your Routine

- Adapting to Changes: Be prepared to modify your workout split in response to changes in your fitness levels, goals, or life circumstances. Flexibility in your approach will help maintain progress.

- Learning from Experience: Both your own experiences and those of others can be insightful. Continually refine your approach based on what you learn about your body and its response to different training stimuli.

In navigating the world of workout splits, understanding these facets is crucial. By gaining clarity on these aspects, individuals can tailor their fitness routines to be more effective, enjoyable, and aligned with

Embracing Your Fitness Journey

The world of fitness and bodybuilding is rich with various methodologies and strategies, among which workout splits have emerged as a key element in structuring effective fitness programs. These splits, each with its unique characteristics and benefits, offer diverse ways to organize training to achieve optimal results. The purpose of this chapter is not only to summarize the key takeaways from an exploration of these splits but also to underscore the importance of choosing a workout split that aligns with one's individual goals, lifestyle, and physical capabilities.

Understanding Splits

Workout splits are foundational to structured fitness programs, providing a systematic approach to training. The concept of a split involves dividing your workout routine to focus on different muscle groups or types of exercise on different days. This approach is instrumental in allowing specific muscle recovery while others are being worked, leading to more efficient and productive training sessions. Each type of split, from full-body routines to more specialized regimens like the bro split or the 5x5 program, caters to different training needs and preferences.

Diversity of Splits

The diversity of workout splits is a testament to the variety within fitness training methodologies. Each split, be it a full-body split, upper/lower split, push/pull/legs split, bro split, or the 5x5 program, has unique characteristics that make it suitable for different fitness goals and preferences. For example, full-body splits are great for beginners or those with limited time for workouts, as they allow for a comprehensive workout in each session. On the other hand, more specialized splits like the bro split or the 5x5 program are tailored for those focusing on specific goals like muscle hypertrophy or strength building.

Importance of Nutrition and Recovery

A successful fitness regimen is more than just well-structured workouts; it also involves proper nutrition and recovery. Nutrition plays a critical role in fueling workouts and aiding recovery. A balanced diet, rich in protein, carbohydrates, fats, vitamins, and minerals, supports muscle growth and repair. Hydration is equally important, as water plays a key role in numerous bodily functions, including muscle recovery. Recovery, encompassing both rest days and sleep, is crucial for muscle growth and preventing overtraining. Each workout split should be complemented with a focus on nutrition and recovery for maximum effectiveness.

Adaptability of Splits

The adaptability of workout splits is crucial in their effectiveness. The best workout split is one that fits an individual's lifestyle, personal goals, and physical condition. This adaptability means that a workout routine can be modified as goals change, as one progresses in their fitness journey, or as life circumstances evolve. An individual might start with a full-body split and later transition to a more specialized split as they become more experienced and their goals become more defined.

Experimentation and Evolution

Experimentation is key in finding the most effective workout split. It's important to try different splits to understand what works best for your body and goals. Personal preference plays a significant role in adherence to a fitness regimen, and experimenting with different splits can help identify what is most enjoyable and sustainable for you. As your fitness level evolves, so should your workout split. Being open to modifying your routine as you progress or as your goals change is essential for continued growth and development.

The Role of Guidance and Self-Education

While a thorough understanding of workout splits provides a solid foundation, the value of professional guidance and continued self-education should not be underestimated. Consulting with fitness professionals can provide personalized advice and adjustments to your workout routine. Additionally, continually educating yourself about new training methods, exercises, and nutrition can enhance your fitness journey, making it more effective and enjoyable.

Embracing the Fitness Journey

Finally, it's important to remember that fitness is not just a destination but a journey. It's about enjoying the process, celebrating small victories, and learning from challenges. Your choice of workout split should not only be about achieving your fitness goals but also about enhancing your overall journey, making it more enjoyable and sustainable. Whether you're a beginner or an experienced athlete, the right workout split can be a powerful tool in achieving your fitness goals while keeping the journey rewarding and fulfilling.

Made in the USA
Middletown, DE
11 April 2025